ST PAUL TRAIL

by

Kate Clow

St Paul Trail is a Turkish Cultural Route
www.cultureroutesinturkey.com

2nd Edition, English, July 2013
ISBN: 978-0-9571547-1-1
Designed, Typeset and Published by: Upcountry (Turkey) Ltd,
www.trekkinginturkey.com, www.cultureroutesinturkey.com
Printed in Turkey by: Sena Ofset Ambalaj Matbaacılık San. ve Tic Ltd. Şti.
Topkapı-İstanbul Tel: 0212 613 03 21 Sertifika No: 12064
Distributed by Cordee Ltd, 11 Jacknell Rd, Dodwells Bridge Ind. Est., Hinckley,
LE10 3BS, Leicester, UK, www.cordee.co.uk

This book is dedicated to members of the Culture Routes Society who have helped develop the St Paul Trail - in particular İbrahim Ağartan and Erdinç Barca - and the enthusiastic and knowledge-able team who developed the i-phone app on this route - Gökhan Göktaş, György Zsiga, Aaron Cederberg and Ahmet Özişik.

And especially to Hüseyin Eryurt, who is the force behind our flourishing society.

Thanks......

The St Paul Trail is Turkey's second long-distance walking route. Unlike the Lycian Way, it has not received any commercial sponsorship.

We still hope that, with the support of the Culture and Tourism Ministry, this route will be the beginning of a European Cultural Route following St Paul's travels through the Roman Empire. In order to further this aim and to preserve this and our other long-distance walking routes, in 2012 the Culture Routes Society was formed. For more information on the society, please see the appendices.

Volunteer workers:

Thanks to the groups of volunteers (from many nations) plus the Turkish guides who initially waymarked the route and those who re-waymarked in 2010. In 2011, Zafer Yılmaz of Gençtur organised and Joseph Fauvre Felix led a group of volunteers who repaired and waymarked the path through the Çandir Canyon. Thanks to them and all helpers.

Trekking guides and agencies:

Thanks to the various agencies who are now operating tours on the St Paul Trail and the guides who work for them. They are our bridge between the route and the walkers who enjoy it. The numbers are steadily increasing and the society is working hard to coordinate with them.

Pension owners and village hospitality:

Unlike the Lycian Way, where local people were used to seeing tourists, the first walkers on the St Paul Trail were a complete novelty. Gradually, local people have got used to seeing foreigners in shorts carrying rucksacks over their canyons and mountains. In response to demand and despite burocratic difficulties, accommodation is slowly opening and more operators are offering holidays on the route. Our aim is to offer the villagers in the small settlements in the folds of the Toros mountains a way to connect with the wider world. We hope that they and their children will benefit financially and culturally and make a living in the villages rather than migrating to the cities.

Environmental:

Like every part of central Turkey, the environment of the St Paul Trail is under perpetual threat from dam-building, mining and road-making. Central ministries have for many years ignored their duty of care for the rural economy, landscape and environment and refused to account to the public for the harm they have caused. Thanks to the NGOs, lawyers, journalists and individuals who are attempting to hold both the state and the holding companies to account. We wish them every success in their depressing and exhausting round of awareness-raising, protests and court cases. They are Turkey's unsung heroes.

Others:

Özgür Özaslan and his staff at the Ministry of Culture and Tourism have for many years supported our work. Thanks to the İsparta Culture and Tourism office, the West Mediterranean development office (BAKA) and the Antalya Promotion foundation (ATV).

Many thanks to George Zsiga, for his hard work on the map for this guide. Loads of thanks to the team who developend the i-phone app - this book is dedicated to them. Special thanks to Serhan Keser for the upkeep of our website, www.trekkinginturkey.com, updated. Thank to Frits Meyst for work on the new website www.cultureroutesinturkey.com. Most of all, thanks to Hüseyin Eryurt, who has picked up the baton and conducted the individual voices of our Society into an inspired chorus.

What the press said:

Each day on the trail was a different landscape.

I basked in the gentle breeze along a high ridge overlooking the blue waters of Lake Egirdir, weaving between massive stone towers along a dirt path lined with patches of wild oregano.

I walked through the spectacular stillness of a thick forest filled with giant junipers and pines. Only a slight movement from a stone spooked me out of my backcountry bliss. The strange rock quickly turned into a tortoise, neck outstretched, glancing up at me as if to say "Watch it, I'm trekking here too."

Transitioning between a vast network of village footpaths, migration routes and ancient roads, the St. Paul Trail is rich with remnants from the past. I felt like I was spit out of a time machine as I walked on square slabs of limestone from a main Roman trade route.

Climbing around the crumbling theater at Selge, I belted out a line from "Julius Caesar."

I passed the crippled arches of a Byzantine church one morning and explored the ruins of a hilltop fort from the Hellenistic period later the same day.

The Spokesman Review, Brad Myers

The St Paul Trail takes you on a journey through majestic scenery on a scale that you will struggle to find in Europe, past Turkey's most beautiful lake and through archaeological sites of Graeco-Roman and biblical antiquity, some grandly excavated, some buried in undergrowth....

In 133BCE, when Rome inherited the Pergamene kingdom, Adada was independent and minting its own coins. Never excavated and never pilfered for building purposes, it is remarkably complete, with three well-preserved temples, a theatre, an agora and market building. Trees grow atmospherically from between ancient Roman stones, and it makes a fine and welcome resting place, as it would have for St Paul.

Minerva, Diana Darke

The heat proved the least of our problems. One afternoon the skies opened, lightning flashed and thunder roared. Some hours later, soaked to the skin, we reached Gölcük, a hamlet of two-roomed stone cottages with wooden roofs, high in the mountains, where we were taken in, dried out before a roaring fire, fed on the local fare of flat bread, cheese and yoghurt, and sheltered for the night. Our welcoming hosts were gatherers of thyme, a wild bounty harvested in these parts in late summer and sold for a decent profit.

Cornucopia, Caroline Finkel

Along its two routes, the St Paul Trail forges its way through a dramatic landscape of deep canyons, waterfalls, cedar forests and limestone peaks soaring to almost 3000m. Weaving through the mountains, it links surviving sections of the Roman road St Paul once trod to Selçuk and Ottoman trade routes and droving paths....

The highlight of a stay in Eğirdir is sitting at a lakeside table, sipping a cold beer and tucking into freshly-caught carp as the sun sinks behind the mountains.

Travel Turkey, Terry Richardson

Acquaint yourself with the rhythms and textures of rural Turkey. Experience a way of life unchanged for centuries. Discover alpine flowers, rare orchids, deep red paeonies.

Sunday Times, Tim Salmon

The sound of bells on lop-eared sheep indicated that we were getting near to a camp. Then the dogs announced our arrival. Grandfather Osman Altıntaş and his extended family had arrived at the traditional yayla pasture only that morning and were erecting the tent that would be their home for the next three months. A stout wooden frame was almost complete, over which would be layered plastic sheeting and woven awnings of coarse black goats hair. Piled around were jars of food, cooking pots, bedding and carpets....

In the Toros mountains, this closeness of man and nature is still strong and to see it is, for me, the greatest joy in following the path of St Paul.

The Great Outdoors, Stephen Godwin

Armed only with faint images from Google Earth and a general knowledge of Roman hydraulic engineering principles, we head off across the Turkish countryside and into a densely forested ravine in search of a long-forgotten Roman aqueduct. After consulting a local farmer, slipping down a series of muddied goat trails lining the embankment and wading knee-deeep in the stream, we have arrived at our destination; the weathered stretch of limestone emerges from the thick brush and arcs across the sky. We scramble up the opposite side, bushwhack our way to the top of the bridge and to what will soon be the newest section of the Saint Paul Trail.

American Trails, Aaron Cederberg

Deep in the western Taurus Mountains of Turkey's Mediterranean Coast, along ancient Roman roads and shepherds' tracks, live the ghosts of St Paul and his followers.

Paul came here intent on preaching to Rome's most influential Asian 'provinces'. Today, that groundbreaking moment converges with the archaeology, history, religion, and folklore of civilisations past and present on the sage-covered slopes and pine-clad hills of southwestern Turkey.

Kate Clow... has recreated the overgrown route taken by St Paul on his missionary journeys through Asia Minor.

The Boston Globe, Lynne Levine

Mustafa Acar led me through the spring-flowering village, all tulips and wild tortoises, to a traditional timber house: animal quarters downstairs, living room on stilts above, with rugged floors, wood-burning stove, and his 86-year-old mother hiding from the mid-afternoon sun under a patterned headscarf......

"Villages in rural Turkey are within a generation of dying," said Kate, who was co-ordinating the waymarking team over the dinner table in a remote Forestry Commission hut. "When the old people die, the villages will die with them. My aim, by waymarking trails and fostering infrastructure, is simply to keep the land alive."

Wanderlust, David Atkinson

About the team:

Kate Clow lived in the UK until 1989, when she took a job selling computer systems in Istanbul. In 1992, she moved to Antalya and started freelance work. This gave her scope to explore ancient roads, which form networks linking the centres of ancient civilisations of Turkey. Convinced that Turkey needed long distance walking routes, she connected a series of old roads to make Turkey's first long distance walking path, the Lycian Way. This route was opened in 1999, and followed in 2004 by the St. Paul Trail, in 2008 by the Kaçkar routes and in 2011, assisting Caroline Finkel, by the Evliya Çelebi Way.

In between researching and writing trekking guides, Kate helped form the Culture Routes Society and develop their website, www.cultureroutesinturkey.com. She continues to promote alternative, sustainable tourism both to the Ministry of Culture and Tourism and anyone else who will listen.

Kate first walked around Eğirdir in 1988 and is planning to eventually retire to a self-sufficient *yayla* in the mountains.

Geörgy Zsiga studied in Budapest to become a cartographer, then spent some 10 years travelling around the globe, writing guide books and drawing maps in between expeditions. In the past few years he started archery and has lived a more settled life, since he is a member of the Hungarian National Team. He is now training to get into the Hungarian archery team for the Olympic Games in Rio. Travelling is still a big part of his life, but nowadays he mostly travels to archery competitions all around the globe.

http://www.facebook.com/georgezsiga

Aaron Cederberg studied journalism and languages in the USA, before starting a course in biology / medicine. The real love of his life is the open sky and wind above the earth and the sport of skydiving. After over 1000 flights, an accident has forced him to take time out to recover. But it has not prevented him from travelling, exploring, trekking, writing and photographing. He not only worked on the photography and layout of this book but also, with Gökhan Göktaş, Ahmet Özişik and Geörgy Zsiga, the i-phone application.

Contents

INTRODUCTION 1

The landscape of Turkey's Toros mountains and lake district contrasts and combines in a jumbled geography of forest, canyon and ridges; the byways resound in history; hospitality is a natural instinct in every home. This combination enticed us to develop Turkey's second long-distance trekking and Cultural Route. The peaks, lakes and valleys on this route offer a different perspective on Turkey from the Aegean and Mediterranean coastlines which draw so many tourists. Unlike the mountains of Eastern Turkey - the fabulous Kaçkar and the Aladaglar which attract adrenaline-fuelled adventure seekers during a short trekking season - the Toros mountains and lake district are easily accessible. Most importantly, the area has a visible, walkable history with some interesting challenges thrown in. St Paul's travels in the area provided the inspiration for this walking route.

Pamphylia, Pisidia and St Paul

The area of this walk comprises the two Roman provinces of Pamphylia and Pisidia. Pamphylia, the coastal strip was rich, hedonistic, hot. Pisidia, in the sharp ranges between the sweltering coast and the colder central plateau, had a reputation for lawlessness. In 46AD St Paul walked north from Perge, the major town of Pamphylia, to Antioch in Pisidia, a Roman *Colonia* / Imperial garrison town and the major city of Pisidia.

Between Perge and Antioch lies wild country. The folds of the Toros mountains are crumpled and creased in a way which offers no natural routes. The rivers, flowing from the plateau to the sea, have cut down through layers of soluble rock to create deep canyons filled, at snowmelt, with torrents of white water. Thick forests have blanketed the valleys right up to the tree-line, leaving stark white limestone peaks rearing their heads above the evergreen hillsides. To the north of the Toros, the hollows in the plateau filled up with natural lakes and malarial marshes, between bands of rolling down-land.

There were roads. By the time St Paul arrived, the country had been settled for well over a thousand years. The main route was the west-east Via Sebaste which ran from the Aegean to Antioch in Pisidia and on to the east. It was augmented by a link-road which ran north-west from Antalya and met the via Sebaste north-west of Lake Eğirdir. That was the long, but safe, way round. The alternative was the direct route northwards, following the Kestros river towards Lake Eğirdir then skirting the lake. The only real difficulty was the short section, a few Roman miles, where the road followed the Kestros through the precipitous gorge of the Yazılı Canyon. We don't know for certain if the Roman road through the canyon had been built when St Paul walked north. If not, there must have been, as today, some way to bypass the canyon on foot.

The route we have chosen may not be that which St Paul walked. It passes cities and settlements which existed in his time and churches which were built soon after. Nobody left a detailed itinerary; nobody today knows; it isn't important to us. What does matter is that this very special area offers a mix of excellent walking country coupled with some well-preserved stretches of Roman road.

To add to the pleasure, the villages that the route passes are huddles of houses which still keep their original purpose and form, whether agricultural or pastoral, summer shelters or winter refuges. The people that remain haven't changed much, either.

Like most of the world, Turkey is experiencing a rapid drift to the cities. The lowering of the water table, caused by climate change, is already taking a toll. The villages on this route may eventually die. That's all the more reason to see them now, while they are still there, before the generation who still live in the old ways are finally consigned to the earth on which they have spent their lives.

Why walk?

As any experienced long distance walker knows, walking gives you time to immerse your-self in the culture of the country; time to stop at rural villages which rarely see a stranger and where the Muslim code of hospitality lives on. In these villages, people still have the courtesy and curiosity to share their food and homes with complete strangers. Their generosity appoints you ambassador at a simple country court.

Walking gives you time to observe. Time to watch the changing light over the hills as the sun rises up the eastern sky. Time to listen to the buzzards calling to each other as they quarter a sun-baked gorge, looking for their prey. Time to hunt down the small snowmelt bulbs, float-ing lightly above the peaty soil. One of the pleasures of this walk is the forests; there are many centuries-old cedars, junipers, planes and chestnuts shading the paths or standing at the stream edges.

Walking gives time to think about the people who trod the route before you, who left their mark on the countryside. There's a lot of history in this book; some of our words may answer your questions but we hope they may prompt you to further inquiry. Even if you are not remote-ly interested in history, you will walk through an area where three thousand years of habitation has been hewn into the landscape. Every pass has its track; every path has its purpose; every place is linked in an evolving physical and cultural network.

The Route

The St Paul Way is a 500km long-distance walking route, also described, from its subject and because of the historical sites along the route, as a Culture Route. It's one of a growing number of long-distance walking routes in Turkey and linked to the Culture Routes Society. The south-west branch of the St Paul Way starts easy and get harder, and the last part, north-east of Eğirdir lake, is easy, but the rest is not - it's best graded as medium to hard. The route is in three sections, so if you want to walk the entire trail, at some point you will need to transfer from one section to another.

The route has huge variety – farmland, forest, mountains, valleys, canyons, cliff-tops, rivers and lakes. The paths range from forestry roads to goat trails. The gradients are rarely gentle; steep ascents and descents are the norm. In the route description we warn about any sections which may be difficult in bad conditions.

You can walk some parts of the route as day-walks; other mountainous sections are difficult to access. The best base is Eğirdir, where you will find organised transport and good accom-modation, but Sütçüler, Barla / Bağören, Çaltepe and Kasımlar / Kesme also have local accom-modation and some transport.

Waymarking and signposts

Like most of the Culture Routes, St Paul Trail is waymarked in red and white paint flashes, according to the following rules:

- there should be a waymark at least every 100m and usually less, especially on difficult paths

- the waymarks are parallel with the route; those on bends are curved to show the direction of the bend

- generally waymarks are on rocks and at a consistent height, but in a few places we have marked trees

- waymarks are visible from both directions; if you appear to be lost it's always worth looking back!

At junctions with roads, the route is signposted with yellow/green signs - these are being gradually renewed. If you find that markings or signs have been damaged or removed, please e-mail us .

This Book

This book contains enough information for independent trekkers with some experience of a map and compass (and preferably a GPS or i-phone), to trek during the spring - autumn season. The first part of the book includes an overview of the history of the area with emphasis on the sites you will see en route, a guide to the environment and the flora of the area. Another useful section is an easy guide to Turkish. Chapters 7-9 describes the three branches of the route in sections, usually of one-day length, starting and ending at places where you can find accommodation, supplies or transport.

The section descriptions include:

- a summary of the section, pointing out any possible problems.
- an altitude diagram showing overall distance and altitude changes (this is not actual distance walked, but computed distance between GPS points; it is about 25% shorter than the actual distance).
- times between landmarks - including stops for photographs, etc., but not longer breaks.
- a route description, running S to N, in very simple language – we have tried to remember that English is not the first language for many trekkers and that some people walk from N to S.
- boxes with description of the villages or places of interest along the route.

We use metres (m) or kilometres (km), temperatures in centigrade, times in hours and minutes, longitude and latitude in degrees and decimals and North/South/East/West are shortened to N/S/E/W. Directions are often given as both physical and compass direction eg. R/N - right/north; L/SW - left/southwest.

i-phone application, *harita* / map and GPS data

There are no readily available high quality, detailed maps of the area, so the Culture Routes Society has just completed an i-phone application to guide you along the St Paul Trail. The maps on this application are far more detailed than the map attached to the book and the GPS signal picked up by the phone places you exactly on the application map. Although you may occasionally lose the signal in canyons or forests, the map in the application has plenty of detail to guide you anywhere. It has summary information about the places along the route, including places to stay, restaurants and shops. It also has an emergency call system, ability to ring ahead to accommodation and bus times.

However, it's not intended to replace the book, which has far more detailed historical information, a map which gives a good overview of the trail and, most importantly, doesn't need a battery or a signal to power it! If you don't have an i-phone, with the password in this book you can download the GPS data which forms the base of the application from our website - the points are accurate to within 10m. As an alternative to an i-phone, this data can be easily loaded to a hand-held GPS. You could also load the GPS points to Google Earth and look at the route before you start. The Google Earth photography of this region is not yet consistently good but most areas were re-photographed since 2010 and are now satisfactory.

Because the trail is waymarked, experienced trekkers could easily walk it with just a compass. However, the i-phone app or a GPS is a safety aid if you want to leave the trail and explore or if you are walking alone. The app gives you immediate information about your surroundings, showing you the nearest water, road or village.

History - local museums and sites

The museum in Antalya is one of the best in Turkey. It contains much impressive Roman-era statuary and sculpture from nearby Perge, the west starting point of the route. The Mediterranean Civilisations Research Institute, situated in a fine period building in Antalya's old city, has a reference library containing antique and modern works on the area. Isparta has a state archaeological museum containing Roman and Byzantine era remains.

Off the route, but worth a trip from Antalya or Eğirdir, the well-excavated Pisidian site at Sagalassos, 7km above Ağlasun, was on the main route N from the coast. This flourishing, well-defended city was stormed by Alexander the Great in 333BC. It later became one of Augustus' Colonia cities so has a newly-excavated complement of Roman buildings. After two earthquakes in the early 6th C AD, the mountain-side site was abandoned and remained undisturbed until excavations started; work has progressed fast and there is much to see.

40km east of Antalya, on the way to the east starting point, is another well preserved but mainly unexcavated Graeco-Roman city, Aspendos, notable for its superb Roman theatre. In June-July and September, it hosts an annual opera and ballet festival; it's worth timing your visit so you can see a performance.

At the start of the route, Perge, chief city of Pamphylia, is a vast open air archaeological museum spread out across the plain, with a well preserved theatre, *stadium*, *agora*, an impressive, huge bath house and a colonnaded main street.

At the end of the trail lies Antioch in Pisidia, high on the Anatolian plateau. Once capital of Pisidia, it has sections of aqueduct, *nymphaeum* and baths, an unusual temple in a huge precinct and the remains of the church of St Paul. The site is still under excavation and the charming state museum at Yalvaç has many of the finds, including a baptismal font with the words 'St Paul'.

Selge, on the east branch of the route, is in a dramatic natural setting above forest and surrounded by rock formations. The theatre is better preserved than the stadium, baths and temple. The position of the present-day village over the ruins adds to its charm.

Pednelissos is an isolated site at the base of a huge rock formation. The original walls as well as a later agora, baths, etc are a main feature.

The other significant site is Adada, where the two trails merge at a wonderful section of old road, which Paul may have walked. Large and small sites on the route are described in the route section.

When to Walk - Climate / *iklim*

The route varies greatly in height (between sea level at Perge and 1800m near Barla), so temperatures and weather conditions can also vary widely. The area south of the Taurus (south of Çaltepe and Sütçüler) has a Mediterranean climate; the peaks form a barrier to winter storms and the southwest wind warms the area in spring. North of this line, as the Toros climb to the Anatolian plateau and the trail rises above 900m, the summers are hot and dry and winters are snowy and windy.

This guide shows average temperatures and rainfall for three locations and two different periods. It should give some idea of when to walk.

We can't tell you when the winter rains will start and stop - climate change now causes so much variation - so you may get caught in unseasonal weather.

The best time to walk the entire trail is in either late spring or early autumn, ie. late April / May / June or late August / September / October. In spring, the mountains above 2000m are still snow streaked, spring flowers abundant and the days warm. Nights can still be very cold and there may be sudden storms, with thunder and lightning, heavy rain and low cloud. By early autumn, the snow has gone, the air temperature is warm and, except maybe for thunderstorms, there is little chance of rain.

You can walk the south part in late January, February and early March, when the coastal weather is warm and sunny and the snowy peaks glitter. The north part of the trail is breathtakingly beautiful at this time, but you will have to cross snow on the passes, some sections may be muddy and you need extra equipment.

We don't recommend trekking in late November, December and January; rainfall is high and the north-east Poyraz wind can bring sudden freezes.

	Lake District	Sütçüler region	Perge
(Altitude)	1750m	848m	90m
Mean annual temperature °C	8.5	13.8	17.8
Average maximum temperature	14.4	19.6	23.7
Average minimum temperature	2.9	10.0	12.6
Total rainfall (mm)	339.3	989.1	902.6
Summer (June-Sept)			
Mean temperature °C	20.0	22.4	29.6
Average maximum temperature	26.4	29.5	34.1
Average minimum temperature	6.0	18.0	17.1
Rainfall in this period (mm)	36.9	100.0	7.9
January			
Mean temperature	-3.4	-2.0	1.6
Average maximum temperature	6.2	4.3	7.9
Average minimum temperature	-2.0	-4.0	-0.1
Rainfall (mm)	34.7	167.4	139.9

Independent Trekkers

You can walk this trail solo, form your own group or join a guided group. If you walk independently, and want to do the whole trail, you will have to bring a tent. Only on a few sections there is sufficient accommodation for you to do several days walking without a tent.

For independent walkers, the newly-formed Culture Routes Society has an office in central Antalya where you can get help with accommodation bookings, advice on transport, leave excess luggage, use the internet and even drink a coffee! See www.cultureroutesinturkey.com.

Guided or Self-guided Holidays

Turkish and European tour operators which offer self-guided or guided holidays are listed on the website. Most guided treks include a mixture of accommodation in pensions and village houses. If you make your own group, most of the companies will provide exactly the itinerary you want, especially if you intend to trek outside the peak season.

In general, it's cheaper to make your own flight arrangements and join a Turkish-operated group at the start of the trek. In Turkish law, all foreign operators have to work with a Turkish operator, so a foreign operator's ground crew and guides will almost inevitably be Turkish. You can initially compare products on the internet and conclude your arrangements by e-mail. Check what equipment (eg. sleeping bags) you need to bring; tents, cooking equipment etc. are almost invariably supplied. Check that the operator's grading of the holiday matches your level of experience and fitness. If you don't know the other group members, ask about their ages and fitness. A group can only travel at the speed of the slowest trekker and a mis-matched group is no fun for anyone.

Self-guided holidays are a new and easier option on parts of the St Paul Trail. If you want to trek with friends or alone, self-guided companies make all bookings, arrange transport and transfer your bags so that you walk with only a day-pack, following a set of notes and a map.

2 PRACTICALITIES

Most people will arrive in the area via the international airport or bus station at Antalya. The old city in central Antalya has many pensions and opportunities for everything from boat trips to concerts, so is a good place to relax after or befor the trek. Buses run frequently from Antalya to Aksu/Perge, the west starting point; the site is about 2km from the bus stop. The connection to the east starting point, at the Roman bridge close to Beşkonak, is slightly more complicated: frequent buses run from Antalya to Serik, a market town on the coast road east of Antalya, then local buses run to Beşkonak, Selge or Çaltepe. There is a bus service from Antalya to the trail's end at Yalvaç. Eğirdir, the largest town along the trail, is a good central hub for short walks - buses run from Antalya via Isparta.

Airlines

National carriers fly to Antalya from most countries in Europe; as well as Turkish Airlines, private airlines such as Sun Express, Onur Air, Pegasus or Atlasjet have scheduled flights to Antalya from European and Middle East destinations. There are also many charter companies, flying especially from Germany, Holland and the UK, which can be considerably cheaper than the scheduled airlines but less flexible in terms of duration of stay. Between Easter and October there is plenty of choice of charter flights but in winter some close their operations. All companies have English-language web sites.

The airport is about 20km from Antalya and 2km from the main E-W road running Antalya - Aksu/Perge - Serik. A local bus runs from the domestic terminal to the bus garage. If you want to go to the city centre, get this bus and change to the tram at Meydan. Taxis to central Antalya or to Perge cost about 15 euros. There are plenty of pensions in Antalya's old town, but if you plan to arrive in the early hours, book first. There are no pensions at Perge.

Train / *tren*

The nearest rail station to the route is at Isparta, close to Eğirdir. The line to İstanbul has been closed for several years and the reopening is not planned for another year or so; the track, laid over 100 years ago, is being relaid. When it reopens, this will be an excellent way to join the route; check our website for information.

National Buses / *otobüs*

Inter-city bus travel is still cheap (from 25 euros for the 750km journey between İstanbul and Antalya), efficient and comfortable. Better companies use brand new, air-conditioned coaches, provide soft drinks, tea/coffee and cake on board and make regular stops at service stations. Since several companies compete, except at peak holiday times, you can get tickets for one or two people at short notice. Most buses leave İstanbul *otogar* / bus station (on the European side) at between 8.00-12.00pm, Harem *otogar* (on the Asian side) one hour later and arrive in Antalya 11 hours after that. Bus companies have city offices in various districts on both sides of the Bosphorus in İstanbul and run shuttle services from the offices to the *otogar*. There are also regular buses from all major provincial towns. Check the website for useful links.

Local buses / *dolmuş*

Local buses run to or from the provincial capitals at Antalya and Isparta; Antalya's local buses mostly leave from the main *otogar*, but Isparta has both an inter-city *otogar* and a smaller one for local buses. Eğirdir, Yalvaç and Sütçüler also have *otogar* with several firms operating scheduled services. Buses going to outlying villages may not use the *otogar* - for example at Eğirdir, many local buses stop on the main road going S, by a line of chemists' shops. Local bus services start from 6.00am and run until late afternoon.

There follows a general summary of these routes; more information is on the website:

Antalya – Serik for Beşkonak – leaves Antalya otogar every 15 minutes during day, stopping at the pedestrian bridge by TEDAŞ on the coast road; returns at similar frequency from Serik otogar. There are daily *dolmuş* services from Serik to Beşkonak, Selge and Çaltepe (except Sunday); they leave from the Çınaraltı café at a roundabout in the town centre.

Antalya – Aksu for Perge. A municipal bus (AC03) runs on 100yıl Bulvarı and the airport road every 15 minutes during the day; returns at similar frequency from under the pedestrian bridge in Aksu. The site is signed from Aksu traffic lights.

Antalya – Gebiz for Akçapınar. Leaves Antalya *otogar* hourly and stops at the pedestrian bridge by TEDAŞ on the coast road. Change at Gebiz for a local *dolmuş* to Akçapınar; it runs several times per day.

Antalya – Yalvaç for Antioch in Pisidia. Leaves Antalya *otogar* daily at 4pm, or you can go at other times via Isparta; returns at 6.30am. Yalvaç *otogar* is southwest of the centre; Antioch is 2km north of the centre.

Antalya – Isparta. Leaves Antalya *otogar* several times per day (several companies run on this route); return from Isparta main *otogar*.

Antalya – Sütçüler. Leaves Antalya *otogar* 5 times per day and returns at similar frequency from Sütçüler *otogar*; some buses pass through Çandır.

Antalya – Kozan junction – Pınargözü. One bus daily at 1pm, returning 6am; leaves from a side-road just N of the Meydan roundabout, returns from Pınargözü shop; not Sundays.

Isparta – Eğirdir – Yalvaç. At least 4 buses per day run via Eğirdir, stopping on Eğirdir main road going S half an hour later. Return buses depart from Yalvaç *otogar* at similar frequency.

Isparta – Eğirdir – Sipahiler – Sütçüler. At least 4 buses per day, stopping on Eğirdir main road going S.

Isparta – Eğirdir – Yükarı Gökdere · Kırıntı · Karadiken – Sütçüler. At least one bus per day, stopping on Eğirdir main road going S.

Isparta – Eğirdir – Kasımlar. Leaves Isparta local *otogar* at 1.30pm daily; 3.00 on Sundays and stops on Eğirdir main road going S. Returns at 6.00am from the square in Kasımlar.

Isparta – Eğirdir – Kesme. Leaves Isparta local *otogar* at 1.30pm daily except Sundays and stops on Eğirdir main road going S. Returns at 6.00am from the petrol station in Kesme.

Isparta – Eğirdir – Yükarı Gökdere · Kırıntı · Çandır. Leaves Isparta local *otogar* at 1.30pm daily and stops on Eğirdir main road going S. Returns from the junction near the Forestry office in Çandır at 6.00am.

Since Antalya and Isparta provinces are separately administered, there is NO BUS that runs the length of the Köprülü Canyon road from Serik to Kesme. Links and further information are on the website. Various inter-village *dolmuşes* run especially to serve schools and markets; see the route section.

Getting to the start

Perge is about 2km north of the main D400 coastal road, 15 km east of Antalya, in the town of Aksu. Get off the bus at the main traffic lights in Aksu, just before the overpass; Perge is signposted. The site is about 2km walk N then E then N, past a post office and a school. There's a ticket booth and entrance charge, toilets and a cafe.

Hitchhiking / *otostop*

In Turkey hitchhiking is expected and welcomed as a way to get to know visitors. Don't hitchhike over routes where there is a frequent bus service, except after the last bus has gone.

But from village to village, it is the most convenient mode of travel and passing vehicles will often stop to offer you a lift. To stop a vehicle, signal by waving your arm up and down, as though you are going to fly.

You may be offered lifts in *kamyon* / lorries, in trucks, or on tractors. The *araba* / cars that sail past will be those with foreign or İstanbul drivers. To prevent misunderstandings, write your destination on a piece of paper and show the driver. Be prepared to enter into simple conversation - your name, home country, where you intend to sleep, etc. Hand round *şeker* / sweets or *sigara* / cigarettes but don't offer money unless the driver stops for *benzin* / petrol, or it is a journey of over about an hour - then you can make a contribution. When you get out, shake hands and wave goodbye.

If you are a woman hitchhiking solo, do it during daylight, away from Antalya, dress respectably with knees and arms covered and make it clear as soon as the car stops that you just want a lift. If your intentions are misunderstood and the driver starts to make any advance at all, demand that he pulls over (everyone knows what 'stop' means) and get out. He will probably apologise profusely and you can forgive him politely.

Hitchhiking can result in invitations to join a picnic, come for dinner or even a bed for the night. See the section on village hospitality and be flexible enough to change your plans a little.

Language

With the exception of the lakeside resort town of Eğirdir, this trail runs through a remote and mountainous region, where tourists are seldom, if ever, encountered. It follows that very few locals you meet on the trail, whether in their villages or on their summer pastures, will speak any English. It is, therefore, well worth learning the key words we have given through out the book, studying the quick pidgin Turkish guide in Appendix 4, and bringing along a dictionary and/or phrasebook. Most locals will adore you for having taken the trouble to learn even a very few basic words and these, accompanied by a bit of sign language and a smile, will usually get you more help than you have any right to expect!

Dogs / *köpek*

The backbone of the local economy is livestock, particularly sheep and goats, and you will encounter many shepherds and their flocks on this trail. The flocks are sometimes guarded by large, fierce looking *köpek* /dogs, (usually the local breeds of Kangal or Karabaş /black head) and it is not a good idea to wander between the dogs and their flock. Having said this, the dogs are nearly always all bark and no bite, and the mere action of picking up a stone and pretending to throw it is enough to keep them away. When approaching a village or nomadic encampment, call out to avoid taking the dogs by surprise. If you are really concerned, take a dog-scaring whistle or alarm.

What to bring and wear

The equipment you require depends on the time of year and which sections of the trail you choose to follow. This advice is for those tackling long sections of the route, especially the higher altitude parts. The first part relates to use of a GPS/i-phone; please read this section. If you are used to walking in remote areas with extreme variations in season and altitude, you will have your own ideas and can skip most of the rest!

The office of the Culture Routes Society in Antalya carries some equipment for sale (eg. gas cylinders, cooking gear) and larger items for rent. Check our website and/or mail us first.

Compass / *pusula*

Even if you are an expert GPS user or have the i-phone app (see below), bring a compass as a backup.

i-phone app and GPS

Waypoints are available for the whole route; they are set up on both the i-phone and the GPS files as a series of routes so you will be guided along the trail from a definite starting point to a finish point. The advantages of using the app or GPS are as follows:

- they give a distance and bearing to the nearest point on the route, so you can wander off the route knowing that you can find your way back
- you know the distance to your target or any other point, so can estimate how long you have to walk
- you're not totally dependent on the map and book; if you lose them, you can still continue
- you're not dependent on the waymarks; if they have been damaged or lost, you can still continue
- most water points are marked so you need carry less safety margin
- you can phone for help, give a GPS location, and know someone will find you
- you can mark any problem areas or interesting finds for future trail users

However, like any other electronic device, they can malfunction, be lost or fall in a river! Test battery life before you start and plan recharging or renewing batteries. For more information about the i-phone app, look for St Paul Guide on the appstore; sample screens are on our website. For technical information about the app, setting up your GPS and loading the routes, see Appendix 10.1.

Banks and Money / *Banka ve Para*

You need to have sufficient Turkish Lira to cover costs of travel, pensions, food plus some for emergencies. Some pensions accept payment in euros or by credit cards. Yalvaç, Eğirdir, Sütçüler and Antalya have ATM's and post offices where you can change foreign currency.

Mobile phones / *cep telefonu* and internet

Turkey's mobile coverage is improving, but is not uniformly good; in the canyons and some forests there may be no reception. You can get a Turkish SIM card with pre-paid units so you can phone or message at local (cheap) rates. Top-up units are available in towns. The brands available are Turkcell, Telsim and Aria; Turkcell is the most expensive but has the best coverage. You may have to 'unlock' your phone when fitting the card; most phone shops in Antalya will do this for you.

There are many internet cafés in Antalya, and many pensions offer their own internet services. On the trail you are limited to a few pensions, or internet cafes in Sütçüler, Eğirdir or Yalvaç.

Camera / *fotoğraf makinası*

The clear air, spectacular views, magnificent scenery, unspoilt ancient sites and the timeless rural way of life make the trail a photographer's paradise. Most local people are delighted to have their picture taken, but you will get more natural pictures by zooming from a distance. Ask before you take pictures, especially of girls or young women - most will allow you to go ahead.

Make sure your case or bag will protect the camera against accidents and rain. Also bring a spare battery or recharger, a wipe and brush to clean off dust, a download cable and a flash disk to take downloaded photos.

Local dress codes / customs

The inhabitants of rural Turkey are traditionally minded, so however much you may want to walk in skimpy shorts and a singlet, please observe the local dress codes. When approaching a village or town, catching a local bus or talking to a goat-herd, make sure that your shoulders, chest and knees are covered. Carry a lightweight pair of *pantalon* / trousers and a loose *gömlek* /shirt that you can slip on or off as required. These will also protect you from sun and wind-burn.

You are certain to be invited into a village house or a shepherd's goat-hair tent for a glass of tea, a cool *ayran* (a salty but refreshing mix of yoghurt and water) or even a meal. Take off your boots or shoes at the door and enter in *çorap* / socks or bare feet - you may be offered indoor sandals or *terlik* / slippers to wear. If you are offered a bed for the night, you will probably sleep in the same room (or in the summer, on the same roof) as members of the family. Like them, you should go to bed almost fully dressed.

Boots and socks / *ayakkabı ve çorap*

You need a good pair of walking boots, with thick soles and ankle support, to protect your feet on the rocky paths and scree; three season leather boots are best. If you intend trekking above the snowline, rigid soled boots are better but heavier. Shock-absorbing inner soles reduce stress on feet and knees; sandals or light camp shoes allow you to relax. Good quality, thick walking socks protect your feet, absorb sweat and help prevent blisters. Gaiters are useful above the snow line, in thorny scrub or mud.

Clothing / *Giyim*

Thin, lightweight clothes allow you to add or take off layers according to altitude, shade or time of day. A base layer polypropylene vest or T-shirt is good for all but hottest conditions. As the middle layer, a fleece provides warmth but also is light and dries quickly. The outer layer should be a windproof and waterproof jacket. From June to September, a lightweight Pertex jacket is sufficient but in spring, autumn and winter, take a heavy-duty breathable jacket with a hood.

Specialist trekking pants made of a lightweight, quick drying but hard-wearing fabric will resist scratchy bushes; zip-off legs are good. Polypropylene thermal tights are lightweight and keep you warm; waterproof over-trousers slip easily over them.

Sunglasses / *güneş gözlüğü* and sun protection / *güneş kremi*

Don't underestimate the strength of the sun, especially in the summer, but also on sunny winter snow slopes. Take good quality mountaineering or skiing sunglasses and a cheaper back-up pair. Take a large cotton scarf, which can double as a towel and sweat-rag. Unless you come from a hot climate, you need high factor sunscreen all year.

Tent / *Çadır*

Unless you plan to stay throughout in village houses or pensions (which is possible on the southern sections of the trail), take a lightweight, free-standing backpacking or mountaineering tent. It should have an overhanging flysheet or sufficient space between the inner and outer tent to allow you to cook under cover. Models where the fly is pitched first are better in rain, as the inner tent stays dry. I use a Mountain Equipment Bugdome weighing about 1.5kg and, in spite of having mesh walls and only a partial flysheet, it has kept me and my dogs dry in heavy rain; I don't carry tentpegs but weigh the tent down with stones.

Backpack / *Sırt Çantası*

To carry your gear, you need a framed or stiffened backpack of 55-75 litres, with a padded hip belt and a chest strap; these will lessen the strain on your back and shoulders. Useful features are clips for walking poles and pockets on the waistbelt or shoulder straps for camera, i-phone or GPS. Backpacks used to weigh at least 3kg – now you can get excellent packs weighing between 1 and 2kg. A narrow pack without side-pockets is less likely to catch on bushes. Bring a waterproof pack-cover so you can leave your pack outside the tent at night. If you bring a poncho, check that it fits over the pack; you may need extra ties to anchor it. Use lightweight, waterproof stuff-sacks for your equipment; pack heavy items as close to your back as possible and put items you may need during the day (first-aid kit, waterproof, etc) in top or outside pockets.

Walking poles / *direk*

Walking poles take the strain off your knee joints and lower back and help maintain balance on scree, snow slopes and stream crossings. They give some protection against dogs. I recommend medium-weight poles with clip adjusters and removable baskets for snow. Photographers can get a fitting for attaching a camera.

Sleeping bag / *uyku tulumu* and mat / *mat*

Take the lightest, best quality three / four season sleeping bag that you can afford. Down bags are less bulky, lighter and provide better insulation than (admittedly cheaper) synthetic bags. However, they lose their 'loft' if they get wet and are more difficult to dry. A silk or thin cotton liner helps to keep your bag clean, provides extra insulation and in very hot conditions can be used on its own.

Self-inflating sleeping mats provide better insulation and are more comfortable than foam mats but puncture easily. A good, but bulky, compromise is a lightweight ¾ length self-inflating mat used over a thin foam mat. Take a basic repair kit.

Bumbag / daysack

If you are backpacking, take a lightweight fold-up daysack for essentials such as cash, this book, notebook, sunglasses and sunscreen. Much of the time it will be stuffed in your backpack, but for short excursions you can abandon the backpack and take only the daysack.

You can also pack unwanted gear into a daysack and leave it at a pension or send it by bus to another point on the trail. Your passport and money are better kept in either a concealed body belt or a secure place in your backpack.

Cooking / *Pişirme*

There is plenty of timber locally, but in summer these forests are tinder-dry and forest fires start easily and can spread rapidly. Therefore only light fires between November and April or during/after rain. Use existing fireplaces and be prepared to put fires out quickly. Never leave a fire smouldering while you sleep.

Camping stove fuels cannot be carried in an aircraft so have to be bought locally.

Gaz / LPG / butane gas stoves are light, simple and clean to use and easily adjustable but they do not burn well in the cold and the cylinder may leak. Screw-valve gas stoves and cylinders are available in Antalya; 190-200 gram (1-2 hours) non-refillable pierce cylinders are available in Antalya and Eğirdir.

Liquid fuel (MSR or Coleman) stoves perform well in the cold or at altitude, but are heavy, slow to set up and dirty to use. *Benzin* / petrol is cheap and fairly easy to find except along the Köprülü canyon between the start and Kesme.

İspirto / methylated spirit (Trangia) stoves are lightweight, efficient and fairly clean but are bulky, not adjustable and don't burn very hot; they are useful for short trips or solo trekkers. *İspirto* is available in small bottles in Antalya or Eğirdir.

Reşo yakıtı /chafer gel burners for barbecues don't burn very hot but are lightweight, reliable and easy to use; they are a useful back-up and will burn for several hours. They are only available in Antalya or Eğirdir.

The basic cooking equipment is a lightweight, all purpose, non-stick pan / *tencere,* a spoon / *kaşık,* fork / *çatal,* knife / *bıçak,* metal mug / *fincan,* matches / *kibrit* and a lighter / *çakmak.* For two or more trekkers, add a kettle / *çaydanlık* or, if you need fresh coffee to operate, a mini Moka pot or traditional Turkish coffee-pan / *cezve.*

Water / Su

Village water is generally safe to drink, and villages have at least one communal *çeşme /* spring or tap (look near the mosque). Many footpaths and tracks between villages have *pınar /* springs or *yalak /* animal drinking troughs near them. You should bring water purifying tablets, but you need only use them if you are forced to draw water from streams or wells which may be contaminated by animals. The water from Eğirdir lake is reputed to be pure enough to drink, but it is safer not to. Only on the higher mountains in summer and autumn may there be a problem finding fresh water.

In hot weather it is very easy to dehydrate, so you should have bottles, Platypus or Camelbak drinking systems holding at least 2 litres. Cisterns or wells don't all have buckets, so take a length of thin cord (5m) and a *kova /* small metal container / bucket to attach to it; plastic buckets float. Use rehydration salts in your water to recover quickly after a hot day on the trail.

Other useful equipment / *üygün malzeme*

Bring swimwear - as well as Lake Eğirdir, you can swim in many places in the canyons and rivers.

A torch (preferably a head torch) is invaluable for pitching/striking your tent in the dark, finding items in your bag/tent at night, following a trail in the dark, or for pre-dawn ascents. It can also be used as a signalling device.

A Swiss Army knife or Leatherman tool can prove useful for everything from cooking and tent maintenance to prising open a lock.

A lightweight nylon cord can be used as a washing line, an extra guy-line in a storm or as an aid to stream-crossing.

A selection of small plastic bottles or containers are useful for cooking oil, salt/spices, matches, etc.

If you intend walking over the higher passes or climbing peaks such as Davraz or Barla between December and March, you should take crampons and an ice axe.

Presents / *hediye*

Take some small gifts to offer in return for a kindness. A handful of sweets, a pen for your hosts' children or a postcard from your country are always welcomed. Show round photographs of your family or home – rural Turks are always interested in life outside their own communities and are obsessed by families. Ask if you can take photos of your hosts and show them the results on the camera. Take an e-mail or facebook address and send them the pictures.

Test before you start

The easiest way to test if you have packed too much gear is to load up your backpack, including food and half-full water bottles, and weigh it. We recommend keeping the weight of your pack down to less than 15 kg for men and less than 12kg for women, though this depends on your strength and endurance! Walk steadily and slowly uphill with your pack at a gradient of 25% for an hour. If you can carry on comfortably with a 10-minute rest every hour, the pack is not too heavy. You'll find that even removing 1-2 kg makes a huge difference. Look out for chafing, uneven distribution of weight and uncomfortable straps and buckles. Make sure your boots are comfortable. Test the pack going downhill as well and finally make sure you can unpack in the dark (make sure the torch is handy!)

Stowing Gear

It is possible to store unwanted items at any of the pensions, the bus garages left luggage / *otogar emaneti* or at the offices of the Culture Routes Society in Antalya. This means you can arrive in the region with excess gear (for example ice-axe and crampons which you need for a summit) and store them in a pension when they are not needed.

Local supplies and shopping

Turkey has several chains of food shops of various sizes. Most Turkish women still prefer to shop from local markets for all except bread, meat and household products. We recommend a visit to a local market at least once in your trek; the variety and cheapness of the food on offer will delight you.

Along the trail, shopping opportunities are limited to the small towns of Kasımlar, Kesme and Sütçuler, plus *bakkal* / small shops in the larger villages, so you should shop in the market towns of Antalya, Eğirdir (Wednesday / Thursday) or Yalvaç (Monday) for major items and fuel.

Bread / *ekmek*

The standard Turkish town bread is a white, crusty oval loaf. Isparta *ekmek*, a round, brown loaf, has a denser texture and keeps much better. Yeastless village bread / *yufka*, comes in large thin circles. You are unlikely to find it in a shop, but village women make great piles every week. You may be given some to take with you on the trail. It can be damped, filled with cheese and onion and fried.

Grains, pasta and pulses

Cracked wheat / *bulgur* is a good trail staple. It is cheap, nutritious, readily available, requires very little cooking and can be flavoured with anything from tomato paste to honey. Rice / *pirinç* is another basic but takes slightly longer to cook. Pasta / *makarna* comes in many shapes; look out for tiny pellets which can be added to soups. Turkish ravioli / *mantı*, small pasta wraps filled with spicy ground beef, are usually eaten in a yoghurt sauce. Lentils / *mercimek* are a useful trail food as (particularly when pre-soaked) they cook quickly. Muesli and cornflakes are available at large markets only.

Meat / *et,* fish / *balık* , cheese / *peynir* and yoghurt / *yoğurt*

Red meat such as beef / *dana*, lamb / *koyun* can be found in butchers in towns but very rarely in village stores. It is expensive and doesn't keep well on the trail. Buy chicken / *tavuk* from specialist shops (which also sell eggs / *yumurta*) in towns and from markets in villages. Burgers, thin sausages and salami are useful but don't keep long. The traditional Turkish *sucuk*, a horse-shoe shaped sausage, is so full of garlic and spices that it keeps for ages; you can fry it with eggs for breakfast or cook it in a stew.

Local cheeses are usually soft, white cow cheeses / *beyaz peynir* with a soft, crumbly texture. Better-quality cheese is more mature, firmer and keeps better on the trail. You could try Diyarbakır *örgü peynir*, a hard white cheese woven into a plait, which can be eaten as it comes or fried. *Tulum*, a strongly flavoured sheep / goats cheese matured in goatskins is delicious eaten with walnuts and *yufka*. Cheddar-like *kaşar* is a hard, yellow cheese which lasts well; matured / *eski kaşar* is more expensive but far tastier and keeps better. Cheese powder called *lor* is useful for flavouring and thickening stews.

Yoğurt is a staple food; *süzme yoğurt*, which has most of the water sieved out, is a thick, creamy paste which can be reconstituted with water, used as a spread or mixed with most other foods; it keeps several days.

Trout is commonly farmed throughout Turkey, and there are a couple of trout farms / restaurants at Çandır. Lake fish (carp / *sazan*) are available at markets and in pensions or restaurants in Eğirdir.

Preserved food / *konserve* and jams / *reçel*

A few tinned items are useful as a treat; tuna, aubergines / *patlıcan* in tomato sauce, stuffed vine leaves / *yaprak dolma*, stuffed peppers / *dolma biber* and dried beans in a tomato and onion sauce / *pilaki* are excellent for picnics or complete meals. Turkey has a wide range of jams and spreads, hazlenut spread /*fıstık ezmesi*, tahini paste / *tahin* and grape syrup / *üzüm pek-*

mez are all useful. Villagers make their own pekmez from local ingredients including mulberries / *dut*, carob / *keçiboynuz* or juniper berries / *ardıç*, and may offer you some. Freeze-dried instant meals are not yet available in Turkey - consider bringing some for an emergency.

Fresh fruit / *meyve* and vegetables / *sebze*

Best brought from local outdoor markets, a wide variety of fruit and vegetables are (seasonally) available. Potatoes / *patates*, aubergines, courgettes / *sakızkabağı*, carrots / *havuç* and onions / *soğan* enliven trail stews, whilst tomatoes / *domates*, cucumbers / *salatalık* and peppers / *biber* are great for picnics. Oranges / *portakal*, apricots / *kayısı*, cherries / *kiraz*, peaches / *şeftalı*, apples / *elma*, pears / *armut*, plums / *erik*, pomegranates / *nar*, water and yellow melons / *karpuz* / *kavun*, strawberries / *çilek*, mulberries, grapes and figs / *incir* arrive at the markets in season. The Lake District has orchards of peaches, apricots, cherries and apples; help yourself to a few in passing.

Dried fruit / *kuru meyve*, nuts / *fındık*

Dried apricots, figs, mulberries and raisins / *kuru üzüm* make great (and healthy) trail snacks, especially when eaten with hazelnuts / *fındık* or walnuts / *ceviz*. Salted nuts include peanuts / *fıstık*, pistachios / *Antep* or Siirt *fıstığı*, almonds / *badem*. Salted and roasted sunflower and other seeds are even cheaper than nuts, as are the roasted chickpeas known as *leblebi*.

Threaded onto string is a sausage-shaped sweet / *tatlı sucuk*. Helva (a tahini based sweet) is available in its plain form, flavoured with cocoa powder or studded with nuts. Less healthy but also good on the trail are the many varieties of Turkish delight / *lokum*.

Sweets / *şeker*, chocolate / *çikolata*, biscuits and cake / *kek*

Pre-packed chocolate, sweets, individual cakes, crisps and biscuits are available everywhere; although peanut bars are sometimes available, muesli and trail bars are almost unknown, so if you want them, bring a supply.

Drinks / *içecek*

Coffee creamer, instant milk powder, teabags (including fruit teas) and instant coffee are available in most markets; you won't find international brands of ground coffee but you can use ready-ground Turkish coffee in a Moka pot. Long-life milk is available in a range of packet sizes. *Ayran*, a salty drink made from yoghurt and water and sold in plastic tubs, is very refreshing and rehydrating in the heat. Instant soups in indivdual packets come in only two or three flavours; there is a huge variety of excellent family-packet soups.

Çay / tea, drunk from tiny, tulip shaped glasses, is served black and usually very sweet. Making a brew is a time-consuming ritual, so you may be delayed while some hospitable villager boils the kettle. The *kahve* / cafe supplies *çay* and *Türk kahvesi* / Turkish coffee; a visit will give you an insight into rural life and the locals the chance to observe the strange ways of foreigners.

Rakı (an aniseed-based spirit like Greek ouzo or French Pernod) is the preferred spirit. *Bira* / lager beer is available in towns and at pensions; the best brand is Efes Pilsen. The most reliable *şarap* / wines include Kavaklidere and Dikmen; taxes are high so wines are fairly expensive.

A trekking holiday is slightly different from the all-inclusive hotel or holiday village type where if you are sick / *hasta*, there is a doctor / *doktor* who speaks your language instantly on call. There is, however, a major hospital with emergency facilities at Eğirdir, and a rescue helicopter based in Antalya. At major hospitals, the care is of European standard. The nursing care is very different, as, like other Middle Eastern countries, the system relies on having a relative or friend stay with the patient in hospital to attend to basic needs.

Chemists / *eczane* and small health centres / *sağlık ocak* can treat injuries, stitch wounds, administer injections, prescribe drugs and refer you to a large hospital if necessary. Doctors in Turkey all speak some English but their proficiency varies. *Eczane* can identify drugs from trade names and supply most medicines and first aid equipment (including antibiotics) over the counter.

If you stick to the route, very little can go wrong, but the temptation to explore is almost irresistible, so read the following:

Before you arrive:

1. Bring a plastic or foil person-sized emergency survival sack. As well as insulating you from cold and rain, you can use it to signal to searchers. Bring spares of anything essential to your well-being - contact lenses, glasses, false teeth, etc, plus sufficient prescription medicine. If you have known allergies or health problems, carry the necessary information in your passport, so in an emergency someone will find it.

2. Buy a health insurance policy including emergency rescue services and repatriation. Take your consulate phone number. If you plan to walk alone for a long stretch, e-mail a copy of your insurance and passport to your consulate so, if you are notified missing, they can initiate rescue services.

3. You will probably be advised that inoculations are required against rabies, malaria and cholera, but the most important inoculation is against tetanus. Malaria and cholera are almost unknown. Rabies is almost unknown in this area; however, rather than spoil your holiday with a course of rabies injections, better have a simple innoculation before you come.

4. Bring a first aid kit, which need contain no more or less than for any other European country - the important items are an effective diahorrea remedy, rehydration salts, treatment for minor cuts, scratches, blisters and stings, an insect repellent, cortisone for insect bites, an all-purpose antibiotic for a sudden flare up of a tooth problem or an infected scratch, and sun screen.

5. If you have previously had an anaphylactic reaction to bee stings or insect bites, bring an adrenaline auto-injector. If you are not allergic and don't scratch, a sting may swell and be uncomfortable for an hour or two, but will soon pass.

On the trail:

1. Whether solo or in groups, do NOT walk in the dark or thick cloud; pitch camp or shelter in a bivvy bag and wait until conditions improve.

2. Pamper your feet! Take every opportunity to check and clean them and your boots, change your socks, add or subtract inner soles, and use the old climbers' trick of resting with your feet above head height.

3. Be alert for dehydration/sunstroke. If all your energy drains away, you feel light headed or dizzy, have a headache or your vision is blurred, you are on the way to collapse. Get into

the shade, cool off by wrapping a wet scarf round your head and drink some water with rehydration salts added. Then rest for an hour or so.

It is also possible to dehydrate gradually over a period of several days. Check how much urine you are producing; if it's less than normal, increase your water and salt intake. GE-Oral is a packaged rehydrant salt mixture available from most chemists.

4. Sunburn is a hazard from May through October. In strong sun, cover your skin, use sun block and renew it regularly. If you burn your shoulders, you won't be able to carry your rucksack.

5. If you get a stomach bug/diarrhoea, try to rest until the bug passes. Eat yoghurt to soothe your stomach and drink rehydrants to compensate for lost salts. If it lasts more than 24 hrs, consider taking a course of Flagyl.

6. If you have not had a rabies innoculation and are bitten by a dog or other animal, try to identify the owner and (if possible) get his phone number. Visit the nearest state hospital or clinic within 24 hours. Owned dogs should be innoculated yearly. If the dog is unidentified or has not been innoculated, the clinic will offer rabies injectons; the service is free. The course consists of five injections spread over a month, so you may have to finish the treatment in your home country; you will be given paperwork for your doctor.

7. Turkey has snakes and scorpions, but they avoid encounters so a bite is only likely if you surprise one. In winter they hibernate, so there's no risk; anyway, most scorpions are too small to do much damage. Make a noise as you walk, shake out your clothes / boots and never walk through undergrowth in sandals. If you are bitten, try to kill the snake / scorpion or at least get a description (snake antidote is species specific). Wash out the wound to remove venom, cover it and if possible immobilise it – if the wound is on a limb, an elastic bandage between it and the heart helps prevent poison travelling through the lymph system. Then get help immediately.

Walking alone

I researched much of this book with my dogs for companions. In my opinion, it is safe for a properly equipped, experienced trekker to walk alone during the warmer months. In case of an accident or missing person, the *jandarma* / rural police will take charge of search and rescue; the problem is deciding when someone is missing. Solo walkers can check in their itinerary and personal details at their consulate so that, in an emergency, someone can notify the authorities. Before your holiday, check the website for further information.

Going for help

If you walk in twos or more, then one person can go for help in case of an accident. If you are the one who has to summon help, and the injury is serious to the point where rescue or evacuation is required, then you need to give accurate information quickly. Before you leave the accident victim, carry out any basic first aid you can, make them as comfortable/warm as possible and leave them sufficient water. Take a GPS point and photos of the area and the injury. Try to send an emergency message or phone someone bilingual. If there is no phone reception and you have to go for help, aim for the nearest village. Use the photos, GPS points and a map to help get your message across. Inform your consulate and insurers as soon as possible; if a helicopter is needed, it will probably have to be authorized by your consulate.

Around Eğirdir, where there is a military base, local commandos have experience of search and rescue and will help in an emergency; in other areas the *jandarma* will carry out rescues.

If this chapter sounds very discouraging, feel reassured by the fact that we have been walking on our own in this area for fifteen years, all the year round, and have never sustained any damage worse than stings, blisters and scratches. None of these have ever stopped us from continuing after a rest.

4   PAMPHYLIA and PISIDIA

The area of the walk, known in antiquity as Pamphylia and Pisidia, was never united under one regional authority. The route, apart from the Pamphylian plain around Perge, runs mainly through Pisidia so the following section concentrates on this area. Hampered by difficult communications in the Toros, Pisidia developed more slowly than the coast; it is still more sparsely populated and less developed.

Outside the major towns, the Toros and the lakes district today support a rural population engaged in agriculture and stockbreeding; the coastal plain around Perge is more intensively farmed. But we know that at the peak of Pax Romana in the 2nd century AD, cities were prosperous and large and, since only a small percentage of the population actually lived in the cities, the countryside must have also been well-populated and farmed well enough to support the city poulation. In places, ancient terracing and waterworks illustrate this. In Byzantine times, political instability kept rural population levels low; they rose somewhat under the Selçuk and Ottoman Turks. The slaughter of the 1st World War probably reduced the population to Byzantine levels. Rural population peaked again in terms of numbers and prosperity in the mid-late 20th C but, since then, migration to the cities has increased and the villages have emptied.

Prehistory

In Pisidia, settlements have been identified dating from about 8,000BCE, the Paeleolithic era. Pottery, obsidian and bronze grave goods show that well before the Iron Age the plateau was occupied and crossed by trade routes. Tilki Höyük, close to Yalvaç, may one day prove to be a major site, but there are many other unexcavated mounds.

From about 1700BCE the Hittites, a people from the north, established a capital at Boğazköy, near Ankara, from which they dominated the central plateau. Cuneiform tablets contain their code of law, which lays down precise rules for governing a mainly agricultural population. Anatolia was rich in metals and the surviving Hittite bronze, silver and iron objects show that the Hittites developed mines; they also invented iron weapons of war, which gave them a military advantage over the surrounding kingdoms. The Hittite site nearest to our area is the sacred spring at Eflatunpınar, between lakes Eğirdir and Beyşehir, where a Hittite water god is represented above a sacred pool. Our area was on the borders between the Hittite empire and a smaller, related kingdom called Arzawa, which included Salawassa, later Sagalassos.

The main craft of the nobles was war and the kings left accounts of their campaigns, mainly against the peoples of the northern Mesopotamian basin, the Hurrians, Mitanni and even the Egyptians. Eventually the Hittite kingdom, under pressure from the north, established a new capital city further south-east. Independent but ethnically related kingdoms continued in western Anatolia, principally at Troy. After the Trojan War, around 1200BCE, Mopsus, Calchas and other leaders founded (or re-founded) a group of new cities in southern Anatolia. Strategically positioned on rivers instead of on the sea, mainly on defensible acropolis hills, many were opposite the rich island of Cyprus, a source of copper and a trading entrepot.

The Phrygians, Lydians and Persians

After the Hittite Empire ended, a people called the Phrygians occupied the central plateau north of Arzawa (now known as Pisidia) but the Lydians replaced them as the dominant power. In 547BCE, the famous Lydian king Croesus, allied with Sparta and the Egyptians, was foolish enough to challenge the huge Persian Empire under its emperor Cyrus; after an indecisive battle, the Persians swept west, occupying all of west Asia Minor and attacking Greece.

The Persians ruled via governors / *satraps*, who were responsible for tax collection but who interfered little with local government and religion. Herodotus lists the tribute imposed by

Darius I, one of Cyrus' successors, as: 400 gold talents from the seaboard Greeks, 500 talents from western Asia Minor; 500 talents plus 360 white horses from the Cilicians but only 360 talents from all the inland areas of Anatolia. This gives a clear idea of the relative wealth of these areas.

Around 500BCE, Darius built the Persian Royal Road from Sardis (near the Aegean) to Susa (in Iran). For the first time, overland communications became important; central Anatolia was coming into its own.

Greek and Persian civil wars

In 499BCE, a rebellion of the Greek city states convulsed the Aegean and the western coast of Asia Minor. The Persians attacked mainland Greece and the islands but were defeated at sea at Salamis and on land at Marathon. Asia Minor remained mainly under Persian control but Greece was divided between the Athenians and Spartans and their allies. In order to dominate smaller states and to oppose the Persians, Athens formed the Delian League; the similar, Spartan-led Peloponnesian League intermittently allied with Persians to attack them. Athens' navy was strong enough to ensure loyalty and collect funds from the majority of coastal Greek cities in Asia Minor.

When Darius II succeeded Artaxerxes in 413, the local Persian satraps intervened in the war. In 408, Cyrus, the king's younger son, was sent west to finance a Spartan victory but, before he reached Sardis, Sparta had won, his father was dead and Artaxerxes II, the older son, had inherited the throne. Cyrus recruited a mercenary army of Athenian soldiers, ostensibly to fight marauding Pisidians, but in 401 marched east to fight for the Persian throne. His Greek commander, Xenophon, describes the campaign in his book, the Anabasis. They crossed Pisidia just north of our route, on their way to the Euphrates, where Cyrus died and the Greek army retreated northwards.

Xenophon mentions that the Pisidians were savage fighters possessing the high mountains between Lycia, Pamphylia and Phrygia. Pisidia commanded two crucial routes – that from the Aegean to the Mediterranean via Termessos and the road north from Pamphylia past Sagalassos to meet the Persian Royal Road; both named cities are west of our route. Xenophon doesn't name any cities in mountainous east Pisidia.

Alexander the Great

In 334BCE, Alexander of Macedon invaded coastal Asia Minor in order to free the Greek cities from Persian rule. According to his biographer, Arrian, his troops marched east from Antalya but were harrassed en route to Perge by a party of Pisidian raiders, probably from Termessos. Perge submitted and paid tribute but Aspendos refused to pay up, so Alexander was forced to take hostages and install a governor and garrison.

Alexander wanted to mount a revenge attack on Termessos but envoys from Selge arrived and encouraged him to march north, over the Döşeme pass, towards Sagalassos, Termessos' sister-city. There, troops from both cities were deployed on the slope in front of Sagalassos' walls. Alexander personally led the guards division in an up-hill infantry charge; they killed 500 defenders and captured the city. Arrian boosts Alexander's reputation thus: 'The Pisidians are all fine soldiers, but the Sagalassians were conspicuous even among a nation of fighters.'

Having subdued Sagalassos, but not other Pisidian cities, Alexander continued north to Phrygia and its capital, Gordium / Yassıhöyük, close to Ankara. In March 333, he cut the famous Gordion knot, so fulfilling the prophecy that whoever could unloose the knot would become lord of Asia. Meanwhile, the Persian fleet had retaken most of the Aegean islands and were provoking muntinies amongst the coastal cities. Alexander took the risky strategy of marching east towards the strategic Cilician Gates, leaving General Antigonus to manage his supply lines through Asia Minor. The strategy worked – Alexander defeated Darius on the Cilician plain, but the supply lines only just held.

After Alexander – the Seleucids

When Alexander met his untimely death ten years later (322), Antigonus, who had saved Asia Minor, laid claim to it. He was forced to fight off Alexander's other generals, eventually losing at Ipsus in Phrygia to Lysimachus. In 282, most of Asia Minor defected to the Seleucids, who had their capital at Antioch on the Orontes (now Antakya). For over a century, the Seleucid monarchy ruled well, encouraging trade and founding new cities, including Antioch in Pisidia, (which was probably intended to control the Pisidian mountains). As Seleucid power weakened, the western provinces of Lycia and Pergamum became first independent then client states of Rome. In 187, after defeating the Seleucids, the Roman Consul Manlius Vulso marched his army across the northern part of Lycia and Pisidia in a punitive campaign so vicious that, on his return to Rome, he was prosecuted for looting.

Pisidian prosperity and Roman inheritance

Pisidians have been typecast as warlike bandits but from the 4th century BC onwards, most of their cities were self-governed by the civilians. After their exposure to the Romans, they gradually acquired massive city walls, Greek-style temples, gymnasia, theatres, agora and public fountains. They became centres of both local and long-distance trade and began to adopt the Greek language. The archaeologist Stephen Mitchell considers them 'a match for anything to be found in the supposedly more civilised areas of western Asia Minor'.

In 133BCE, Rome inherited the Attalid kingdom, which became the large province of Asia, extending from the Aegean to Pamphylia and Phrygia. It had an outlet to the Mediterranean via a north-south road across Pisidian territory, from Afyon / Celaenae to Antalya via Burdur lake and the Döşeme pass. In north-central Anatolia a new Celtic province, Galatia, was formed - Pisidia was now nearly surrounded and kept under control through threats and diplomacy.

During the Roman civil wars, the overstretched Marcus Antonius offered Galatia to Amyntas, a local ruler, on condition that he pacified the area. Amyntas extended his kingdom south to include Pisidia, Isauria and Pamphylia, forming a buffer state east of the province of Asia. According to Strabo: 'Holding Antioch in Pisidia, a section of Phrygia as far as Apollonia / Uluborlu and Lycaonia (to the east), Amyntas attempted to remove the threat of the Cilicians and Pisidians who were overrunning the country. He captured many places which had previously been impregnable.' He probably re-fortified the places he captured, because the city walls at Cremna, Pednelissos and Adada date from this period.

Roman *Coloniae*

The Roman civil wars concluded in 29BCE when the victorious Augustus became first Emperor and adopted a policy of benevolent and peaceful rule. After Amyntas' death in 25BCE, Augustus placed Galatia under the rule of civilian governors, who delegated the running of the cities to the wealthier, landowning citizens. The governor's job was to continually tour his province judging court cases and collecting taxes. As client kings died, the frontier province of Cappadocia was incorporated into the Empire and the Roman boundary stabilised at the Euphrates, where garrisons secured the frontier.

The Emperor founded *colonia*, purpose-built settlements of retired soldiers; in particular, the three *coloniae* at Antioch / Yalvaç, Iconium / Konya and Lystra were militarised cities controlling the mountain people of Pisidia and Isauria. *Coloniae* used Latin, the language of the army, in contrast to civilian Greek; inscriptions found in Antioch are nearly all in Latin. They usually had extensive buildings endowed by or dedicated to the Imperial family, who were now worshipped as gods, especially in the provinces. Those at Antioch included an Imperial cult temple and triumphal arches celebrating military victories.

Roman roads

Roman roads followed a uniform pattern throughout the empire, being either cut in bedrock or paved, laid out to a standard width and with maximum gradients suitable for an ox team. Stone bridges spanned the rivers – examples still exist in the Köprülü Canyon. Higher grade roads, laid out and maintained by the state, were surfaced with local stone or gravel, marked with milestones and often named after the censor who commissioned them. Military garrisons ensured the safety of travellers; wayside inns provided lodging and food. The roads were used firstly for speedy transit or supply of the military and secondly for the transport of produce to the coast for shipment to Rome. Lesser roads built by private individuals linked private estates to the major roads; village roads, which may have been constructed or maintained by local magistrates, linked settlements in the countryside.

South Anatolia's most famous road was the Via Sebaste, which ran from the Aegean, passing north of Lake Eğirdir to Konya and further east. It was linked to Antalya by the north-south road across Pisidia and over the Döşeme pass; it is still visible for many km in this area.

St Paul in Pamphylia and Pisidia

In 41AD, Paul landed in southern Asia Minor on his first inland journey, probaby with the intention of travelling to Antioch in Pisidia, for the Governor of Cyprus, whom he had met, was from that area. Like most ancient travellers, as far as possible Paul travelled by ships plying the coast; an easier and quicker method of travel than walking. He may have landed at Attalia (Antalya) and certainly stayed at Perge, from where he probably took the direct road up the valley of the Kestros towards Antioch in Pisidia (the route via the main roads was far longer). The road crossed the river near present-day Çatallar and probably bypassed Pednelissos, following the river past Çandır into the Yazılı Canyon, where there are Greek inscriptions on the canyon walls. The paved road continued to Adada and up the Aksu river towards lake Eğirdir, which was then two separate lakes. Paul may have walked west of the first lake then turned east across the causeway between the lakes to Antioch; later a monastery was founded here - on what is now the island of Limenia, just off the route.

Decline of Pisidia

In the late 1st and 2nd century, the Roman Empire became prosperous and expanded westwards. By 132AD, when Emperor Hadrian visited, the cities of Asia were enjoying a building boom; more public buildings were erected specially for his visit. Hadrian was worshipped as a god, sometimes in conjunction with Zeus, and dedications to him appear regularly.

As the 2nd century waned, so did Pax Romana; public works suffered from earthquake damage and pirates preyed on shipping. In 259, in response to Sassanid raids, the Emperor Valerian led a huge army across the Euphrates but, near Urfa, they was defeated and the Emperor captured. In 262 the Goths invaded Lydia and Paphlagonia from the north, cutting the major roads and preventing trade. As Sassanid raids penetrated the Mediterranean coast as far as Anamur and Laranda in Pamphylia, many cities reinforced their defensive walls and garrisons. The Romans based a fleet at Side to defend merchant shipping passing along the coast of Pamphylia to Rome. In the reign of Aurelian (270-75) the Sassanid invaders reached Ankara; Roman troops marched from Side through the Taurus to attack them.

In the reign of Probus, (276-82) an Isaurian bandit chief called Lydius ravaged Pamphylia and Lycia. According to Zosimus, an early Byzantine writer, a Roman army under Governor Terentius Marcianus cornered then killed Lycius in the city of Cremna. The Romans assigned captured land to veterans and required all young men to serve in the army, thus preventing them from becoming brigands.

Christianity in the Empire

In the 4th century, under the Emperor Constantine, Christianity replaced the Emperor cult and other pagan religions as the official Roman religion. The Emperor tightly controlled the religious administration, appointing the Patriarch of Constantinople and presiding in person at church councils. When, in 361, the pagan Emperor Julian tried to revive the old religions, he was faced with a popular revolt; the common people were now attached to Christianity. In 385, the Holy Roman Empire was divided into East and West under separate Emperors and rival Patriarchs; a few years later paganism was outlawed. Bishops began to be appointed and the first churches constructed in the cities. Some were converted from basilicas or other public buildings, some richly decorated with marbles and frescoes. Existing temples were not initially converted to churches; they were considered possessed by evil spirits.

Asia Minor was divided into four themes or provinces, each with its own army and naval defence force; our area was included in the theme of Anatolikon. To each theme, the Patriarch of Constantinople appointed metropolitan bishops who governed the city bishops. At the Council of Chalcedon (541), church doctrine was tightly defined and dissent declared heretical, thus alienating the eastern Monophysite Christians, who later converted readily to Islam.

Gradually, lacking finance to govern properly, city governments handed control to the church, which had sufficient income to implement a form of social welfare, feeding and providing shelter for beggars and the old, treating the sick and attempting maintenance of public buildings.

The example of hermits, who, from the 4th century, retreated to the deserts of Sinai, led to the development of monastic orders; Caesarea / Kayseri was the leading centre in Asia. Wealthy patrons endowed many monasteries in order to provide secure, tax-exempted bases for their heirs. Monasteries expanded so fast that the population seems to have fallen - this resulted in a reduction of the area under cultivation and shortage of manpower for the military. The monasteries were often centres of political and religious dissent from the authority of Constantinople and the bishops, but many superb manuscripts, including hagiographies of martyrs and saints, originated in their *scriptoria* / writing rooms.

Decay of the Empire

From the 4th century, as the Empire was unable to maintain coastal security against pirates and raiders, the inland cities became more important. In 365, an earthquake ravaged Pamphylia, destroying the Aspendos bridge and aqueduct. When, in 518 and 528, Pisidia was struck by earthquakes, Sagalassos was seriously damaged and other cities also suffered. From 542, bubonic plague broke out in Empire-wide epidemics, killing between a third and a half of the urban population. Aqueducts, baths and other public works were no longer properly maintained and harbours silted up, so malaria became rife and caused the abandonment of many cities, especially in warmer, coastal areas. Brigands, raiding from poorer states in the east and north, especially Isauria, attacked the cities of Pamphylia and Pisidia. In response the townspeople constructed new city defences, re-using older materials and enclosing much smaller areas suitable for the reduced population. The Emperors tried to defend the area from bandits but their generals looted in order to pay the troops. Rural land was turned over to livestock; animals required less manpower than grain farming and could be moved out of the way of raiders.

Rise of Islam

The Roman-Byzantine Empire was now faced with a series of attacks from the east. First the Persians attacked Constantinople but, in 628, the Emperor Heraclius defeated them and recaptured Syria and Palestine. Only 8 years later, Arabs, newly-converted to Islam, recaptured Palestine and a few years later invaded as far as Constantinople. War was waged at sea; in 655, in the bay of Finike, the Arabs, favoured by superior strength and onshore winds, wiped out a huge Byzantine fleet. The frontier settled at the Euphrates but raids continued annually.

The 8th century was a period of religious controversy as succeeding emperors ordered first the removal of religious icons then their restoration. The Bishops Sisimos of Perge and Basil of Pisidia acted as advisors to the Emperors at various church councils, speaking for or against icons as the political tide changed. Civil wars weakened the Empire and the victor, Constantine V, though a good general, was unpopular. In an attempt to co-ordinate defence, he reorganised the themes, splitting Anatolikon into three. He replaced the locally-funded theme armies with new, centrally paid forces, consisting of up to 30,000 foot-soldiers and 5 - 10,000 armed cavalry, each man supported by a squire and spare horses.

His new policy was to allow fast-moving Arab raiders to penetrate the central plateau; as the raiders passed secure military bases, Byzantine troops harrassed them. As they withdrew, encumbered by loot, the army ambushed them. This policy was not popular with the civilian population, who had to suffer these onslaughts, nor with the ruling classes, who had to pay the new army. With many able-bodied men and women in the church or monasteries and Arab raids destroying crops and livelihoods, peasants were often unable to pay taxes and became de-facto slaves to the larger landowners.

Our area of Pisidia and Pamphylia was usually bypassed but, in 713, Antioch was destroyed with a loss of 30,000 lives and many more captives. The traveller Ibn Khordadh Bey says that, in 840, only five cities remained in Asia Minor – Ephesus, Nicaea, Amorium, Ankyra and Samala, and one of these (Amorium, just north of Antioch) had just been destroyed. From the 7th century to the mid 9th century there was practically no new building of towns or monasteries.

Byzantine revival

In 878, the Paulicians, members of a rebellious sect named after St Paul, who occupied a frontier zone based on Tephrike / Divriği, were partly destroyed; the survivors were forcibly moved to the Balkans. This marked the start of an internal consolidation of the Empire. By the start of the 10th century, Byzantine generals were able to prevent the annual Arab raids. Melitene / Malatya and Edessa / Urfa were recaptured and the eastern frontier secured. Armenia became an ally and contributed troops to the enlarged army which, in 969, recaptured the great fortress city of Antioch on the Orontes. In Constantinople, trade redeveloped; government alternated between the old Constantinople aristocracy and Armenian and other military commanders. In the 10th century, provincial civilian governorship merged with the army command under one commander. Basil II was able to consolidate the Empire within boundaries stretching from the Caucasus to Italy.

Byzantium and the Selçuks

In 1025, after Basil's death, the empire was confronted by the Selcuk Turks in the east, Bulgarians in the west and Normans in south Italy. As it slumped into disorder, a succession of Emperors appealed for practical help from the Pope. Byzantine clergy would not make concessions to Rome on doctrine and, in 1054, both sides' intransigence resulted in a final split between the Roman and Greek Orthodox churches. A few years later, commanding a huge but unreliable army, the Emperor Romanus Diogenes met the Selçuk Turks in battle at Manzikert, but part of his army deserted, he was captured and Byzantine forces effectively disbanded.

The Selçuks originally had no intention of overrunning Asia Minor; their attentions were firmly fixed on the granaries of Egypt. So in 1073, when Alp Arslan won the battle of Manzikert, he did not press home his advantage but demanded tribute and left. The scarce records mean that what happened next is unclear, but a subsidiary clan of the Selçuks led by Kiliç Arslan, along with Danişmendliler, Saltuklu Beylik and Mengüçoğulları clans overran the central east plateau, with, in their vanguard, various Turcoman tribes. The tribesmen even penetrated as far as the Aegean, whereupon some of the Greek Christian population of Phrygia retreated to the Balkans. With almost no army left, the new Emperor, Alexis Comnenus, was pushed back towards Constantinople. The Selçuk Empire occupied all the Anatolian plateau; the Danişmendliler settled down in the Erzurum area as subjects of the Selçuks and the Armenians, displaced by the movement of the Selçuks, settled in the area of Cilicia.

In 1078, when the dust settled, the Selçuk Sultan Kılıç Arslan had established a new capital at Nicaea / Iznik, very close to Constantinople. Alexius Comnenus ruled only parts of western Asia Minor and most of the Balkans; Apollonia Sozopolis / Uluborlu, north west of Eğirdir, became a Byzantine frontier fortress. Alexius also robbed himself of a major tax source by granting duty-free trade rights to the Venetians in exchange for meagre military support, so ruining the finances of the empire.

The Crusades

In desperation, Alexius appealed once more to the Pope for financial help against the infidel. To his dismay, instead of funds, in 1097 the knights then the masses of the 1st Crusade arrived in Constantinople. They defeated the Selçuks at Nicaea then marched across Asia Minor to capture Antioch on the Orontes and Jerusalem. The Selçuks built a more secure capital at Konya, from which they still held much of Anatolia; Byzantine Antalya was cut off from Constantinople. After Alexius' death in 1118, John Comnenus took to the field, reopened the Via Sebaste and captured Beyşehir. The 2nd Crusade crossed the Bosphorus in 1148 but the Selçuks defeated the German contingent at Dorylaeum /Eskişehir. The remaining troops marched to Antalya, where the leaders took ship for Antioch on the Orontes while their men struggled along the coast towards Syria, continuously harrassed and suffering severe losses throughout their march.

The Selçuk kingdom consolidated around the new capital and, in 1176, under Kılıç Arslan II, defeated a Byzantine army at Myriocephalon, again pushing their frontier towards the Aegean. The 3rd Crusade passed through Selçuk territory to Antioch in Pisidia, continued to Konya without beseiging it and crossed the Toros to Seleucia /Silifke, where their leader Frederick Barbarossa died of heart failure and the troops dispersed.

In 1204, the 4th Crusade was induced by the Venetians to sack Constantinople for quick profit; the destruction and loss of life was enormous and many artistic treasures were taken to Venice or other European cities. Byzantium was reduced to an outpost around Nicaea and another in Greece. Kılıç Arslan II's son Keyhusref I, who had been deposed by his brother and was a refugee in the Byzantine capital, took advantage of the confusion and his brother's death to return to Konya and become Sultan again.

Selçuk rule in Anatolia

After Myriocephalon, Apollonia Sozopolis / Uluborlu changed hands and became a major Selçuk stronghold and seat of Keyhusref I. In 1207, he first attacked Isparta, took it after a siege, then marched on Antalya. After a three-day sack, the Selçuk leader Ertoküş was chosen as governor of the city; he endowed mosques both there and in Uluborlu. In a subsequent battle on the Maeander river, Keyhusref I was killed, reputedly by Laskaris, the Emperor of the Byzantine state of Nicaea. In 2011 a truce was concluded and the frontier between Selçuk and Byzantine lands stabilised until the 1260's.

The next Sultans were able to capitalise on this and develop their kingdom. Kaykavuş made trade arrangements with the Venetians and a treaty with Cyprus which left Antalya as a free port. His successor Alaaddin Keykubad made Alaiya / Alanya an important naval and winter base. He built himself a palace at Kubadhabad in Lake Beyşehir and several hunting lodges, including one near Antalya. The Selçuk Empire had now reached its maximum extent, stretching from the Black Sea to the Mediterranean and east to Armenia and Edessa /Urfa.

Life in Selçuk Anatolia

Most of the rural population of central Turkey preferred the lower tax rates under the Selçuks to Byzantine rule. The monasteries were permitted to continue managing their own lands and there was little pressure on the peasants to convert. There are records of bishops in Pamphylia Secunda until the late 13th century. The traveller William of Rubruck, passing through in about 1254, says that there were 10 times as many Christians as non-Christians. He heard Persian, Arabic, Turkish and Greek spoken, with Persian as the court/government language, Greek as the language of the church and Arabic as the language of the mosque and law. Some clans, such as the Karamanoğulları, were Christian but spoke Turkish.

Most Selçuk Turks were traditional pastoralists with sheep and goats, trading in wool and textiles; a separate group, known as *ağaçeri,* probably ancestors of the present-day Alevi *tahtacı,* harvested timber and pitch. Trade was mainly in the hands of Greeks and Jews; central Anatolia was known for timber, pitch, carpet weaving, saddlery and soap; apricots, fine wool and embroidered fabrics were exported.

By the mid 13th century there were 100 towns in Anatolia, of which 24 were metropolitan centres with governors, judges and markets; most were on the site of Byzantine and Roman towns and kept a modified form of the old name.

Main roads ran between the important inland cities of Uluborlu and Beyşehir and the coast at Antalya and Alanya; the old Via Sebaste main road was still in use. The construction of fortified *kervansaray /* travellers' inns encouraged trade on all the main routes. They provided a maximum of three days free board and lodging to merchants and their train and supplied post horses for the Sultan's messengers. Trade was revolutionised by the introduction of camels, which could carry far greater loads than mules for similar amounts of foodstuff and could cope with steeper, narrower roads through the mountains. The ox cart was kept for use on the plains.

One surviving *kervansaray* in our area is the Ertoküş Kervansaray, 30km from Eğirdir, by lake Eğirdir on the Konya road at the village of Yeşilköy. It is now newly restored to its original height. Built on the standard plan, it has a symmetrical *avlu /* hall with arched rooms opening off. One of the entrance doors is flanked by two narrow niches with inscriptions. According to these, Mubarezettin Ertoküş built the kervansaray in 1233 AD.

Mongol overlordship

Around 1240, mounted Mongol forces moved westward from central Asia, driving the Turcoman tribes before them. Amazingly, during the harsh winter of 1242-3, Baiju Noyan's Mongols took Erzurum, the key to northern Turkey, from Sultan Keyhusref II, and in June the entire Selçuk army was lost at the battle of Köşedağ. The Mongols demanded large sums in tribute from Keyhusref's three young sons. The sultanate was first split between two of them, Kiliç Arslan IV and Kaykavuş II, then the third, Keyhusref III, became the Mongols' nominal ruler. Bands of Turcomans, rebelling against the Mongols, appealed to the Greater Selçuk Sultan Bayburts who, in 1277, captured Konya and set up a short-lived rival sultanate. The Mongol armies re-took and pacified the Taurus, ruling through Keyhusref III in Konya and small Turcoman Beyliks in less accessible areas further west. In 1291-2, after Eşrefoğlu and Karamanıd revolts around Uluborlu and Denizli, the Mongols massacred the male population and enslaved 7000 women and children. Finally in around 1305, the Selçuk Sultanate ceased to exist and, by 1335, Mongol holdings in north Anatolia were reduced to a rump around Sivas. The Turcoman tribes had taken over effective government of western Anatolia.

The Turcoman kingdoms - the Eşrefoğulları

The Hamidoğulları and the Eşrefoğulları clans dominated our area. The Eşrefoğulları, under the powerful Seyyfeddin Suleyman, were based in Beyşehir. Shams al din, the inspiration of Jamal al din, founder of the Mevlevi *derviş* movement, dedicated two books on philosophy to this Suleyman. Around 1288, he built a citadel at Beyşehir to protect the city, which had 31 shops, 2 *hans* and a textile market. But in 1292, the Eşrefoğulları, who had allied with the Karamanıds from further east in support of Turcoman independence, suffered the Mongol revenge described above. Later, as they recovered, in 1297-9 they built a magnificent forest-of-columns mosque and *medrese* at Beyşehir.

In 1302, Mubariz al din Mehmet succeeded his father, paid tribute to the Mongol overlords and added Akşehir and Bolvadin to his possessions. In 1326, Timurtaş, a Mongol governor in revolt from his masters, took Beyşehir. Mubariz al din Mehmet was executed and Eşrefoğulları territory partitioned between the Hamidoğulları and the Karamanıds.

The Hamidoğulları

The Hamidoğulları were based first in Uluborlu; Hamid Bey, lord of Uluborlu, participated in the taking of Antalya and probably ruled it from about 1280. Around 1300, he extended his rule to include Yalvaç and much of Pisidia and transferred his capital to Akrotiri / Eğirdir, which took the name of Felekbar. Felekeddin Dundar Bey, his successor, was forced to pay the Mongol İlkhanids 4000 *dinars* per year in tax.

In 1316, the Hamidoğulları, with an army of 15,000 foot-soldiers and 5000 cavalry, captured Aydın and Saruhan. İlkhanid troops pursued them to Antalya and, after his nephew Mahmud surrendered him, in 1324 Felekeddin was put to death. But the clan kept control of Antalya and soon after they took the towns of Beyşehir and Şeydişehir from the Eşrefoğulları.

In 1331, at a time of reasonable prosperity, the writer Ibn Battuta visited Felekbar; he reports on a Mevlevi *derviş* convent, the tomb of a saint, Baba Sultan, the Dundar Bey *medrese* and the Hızır Bey mosque. He also describes markets, rivers, forests and gardens and says that the town was bigger than Burdur or Isparta. The prosperity was soon interrupted by an unsuccessful attack by the Karamanıds; but they were forced to retreat.

A generation later, the power of the Hamidoğulları started to wane; in 1365, they lost Antalya to the Christian King Peter of Cyprus; some time after 1373, they sold Yalvaç, Karaağaç and Beyşehir to the Ottoman Sultan Mehmet 1 for 80,000 *dinars*. The Hamidoğulları provided the Ottomans with 1000 archers for use in Syria and fought on the Ottoman side at the battle of Kosova in 1389, but soon after the clan faded away and their remaining lands were divided between the Karamanoğulları and Ottomans.

The Ottoman Empire

The Ottoman Empire grew from a border principality based on Bursa (around 1300) to command the whole of Anatolia, the Balkans, the Middle East and Egypt (around 1600). Well-organised, mobile military forces permitted such a speedy expansion. The Ottoman policy was not to interfere with the existing religion and social organisation so, by governing with a light touch, were able to keep newly conquered states under control. They organised a feudal system, awarding conquered land in exchange for military service and transplanted groups of peoples from their native lands to points in the empire which had need of population or specific skills. They later levied the *devşirme* (forcible recruiting of Christian boys for palace and military service); this ensured that many Christian families had a protector in the army or palace and therefore an interest maintaining the status quo.

This policy was perfectly satisfactory as long as the boundaries were expanding. As the extent of the empire was limited (it collided with the military powers of central Europe and expansionist Russia), there were no new military fiefs to grant and, by European standards, the military now seemed unprofessional. Nationalist movements, sometimes inspired by European powers, encouraged internal dissent and rebellion. In addition, by concentrating on the military, the Sultans had allowed trade to pass to the Italian republics, which often held monopolies on specific goods, control of ports or coastal forts and owned much commercial shipping.

The practical result was that from around 1600 land holding became concentrated in the hands of powerful families who often extracted as much wealth as they could from the peasant farmers and lived in Constantinople on their profits. Local manufacture and trade was often in the hands of minorities such as the Armenians and Greeks. Muslim peasants lived from agriculture and some basic handcrafts, often moving with their animals from winter to summer pastures in search of fodder.

Eventually, the loss of Greece, Egypt, most of the Balkans and the Crimea reduced the Ottoman Empire to Thrace, the Anatolian heartland plus the Middle East; more was lost during the First World War and new, limited boundaries imposed by the Great Powers.

Ottoman Pisidia

A list of exports from the port of Antalya, which the Venetians captured in 1472, included timber (from the Taurus) slaves (traded with pirates), wool (from inland flocks), carpets (in brilliant reds and blues, made from local wool), saffron (from the saffron crocus, a local crop), sesame (a cultivated plant), gum adragant (also cultivated), gall nuts (collected from oak forests) and honey (a local crop). The list gives some idea of the activities in the hinterland. Later we also know that opium was grown around Davraz and, as today, in other areas. Records of 1522 show that Eğirdir was declining at the expense of Isparta; Isparta had 446 houses against Eğirdir's 335 (including 50 Christian households). Agios Stephanos, the church on Yeşilada at Eğirdir, dates from around this time, as does a church in Isparta. In 1579 Isparta, sometimes known as Hamidabad, became a provincial capital, but later the province was amalgamated under the governorship of Konya.

From around 1600 brigandage flourished – a local peasant hero, known as Katırcıoğlu (the muleman's son) raided trading caravans and gave the funds to the poor. At this time there were very few permanent villages but some 3000 families living in tents around Eğirdir, so there were plenty of places to hide from the authorities. Eventually, in 1710, the central government decided to exile the undesirables to Cyprus but, having set sail from Antalya, the exiles took over the ship and sailed back again.

In 1743, there was a serious earthquake centred on Antalya; the coast was inundated by tidal waves and not a minaret was left standing as far north as Burdur. Following the earthquake, plague broke out and central government lost control of the province. In 1765, Eğirdir itself was beseiged by bandits. The province still produced wheat which, as Egypt became independent, was needed to feed İstanbul; however the merchants of Antalya defied the government and exported it elsewhere for a better price. The 19th century saw three major earthquakes in the Dinar and Isparta areas, followed by another in 1914.

Minorities and Majorities

Overall, it's estimated that only some 300,000 Turks entered Anatolia following the battle of Manzikert, dispersing into the existing population of 3 million. We know that in many areas the monasteries continued to function for centuries and, in spite of legislation forbidding the construction of new churches, they were built in Eğirdir, Isparta and many other places. It was in the interests of Imperial authorities to maintain a Christian population. They were a depository for skills such as metal work (Armenians), money-lending and trade (Jews) and shipping and fishing (Greeks). These *raya /* minority groups paid a special monetary tax which exempted them from military service. Since many taxes were paid in kind, taxes collected in cash were an especially versatile and valuable revenue stream.

Today, it's impossible to know accurately the religious and racial mix in our area during the Ottoman Empire; however, it's estimated that the proportion of Christians to Muslims decreased from over 60% (when the Ottoman Empire was founded) to 10-20% (by 1914). Christians were concentrated in particular villages such as Barla, although there doesn't seem to be a direct link between centres of Byzantine population and late Ottoman Christian population.

To give some idea of the proportions, surviving records from a census show that in the 1840's Isparta had a population of 12-15,000 Muslims, 3500 Greeks and 150 Armenians. Soon after, encouraged by the Great Powers' guarantees of legal self-government and valuable tax breaks, some Greeks returned from newly-independent, poor Greece to Anatolia to take advantage of easier trade opportunities there. From 1880, missionaries funded many new churches, which helped make the minorities more visible.

The end of the Empire

The final century of the Ottoman Empire saw its violent erosion and subsequent collapse. With the support of European powers and the Russians, Christian minority groups claimed their own national states. As Ottoman armies in the Balkans were defeated, many Muslims fled east to Anatolia; others were driven west from the Caucasus. An attempt at democratisation didn't last long and the Sultan resumed direct rule. In 1908, part of the army, supported by minority groups, marched from Thrace to İstanbul and reestablished parliamentary government led by the political party called the Committee of Union and Progress. The Empire was hard pressed by creditors who wanted political concessions for minority groups and, from 1912, wars in the Balkans resulted in the loss of nearly all the Empire's European territory. The Committee began to govern directly, seeking help from abroad to stabilise the situation, but an incident in Serbia resulted in the First World War. The Ottoman Empire entered the War on the German side; it suffered horrendous military losses on the Russian front and at Galipoli / Gelibolu. The first peace agreement, the Treaty of Lausanne, confined the Turks to the central area of Anatolia. A second military resistance movement, later the Republican government, deposed the Sultan and pressured the occupying powers into leaving Turkey.

Republic

The War of Independence raged around the north of our area; Afyon was headquarters for the advance against the Greeks who had invaded from İzmir. Under a second peace treaty, in 1923, Greece and Turkey exchanged an estimated 700,000 Muslims from Greece for about 1,100,000 Anatolian Christians. This, with the tremendous loss of life caused by the war, left a residual population of only about 3 million in the whole of the new country of Turkey. The lifework of the Republic's founder, Mustafa Kemal Atatürk, was to rebuild a nation of mainly women and old people, survivors of the devastation of the Great War. By the time he died in 1936, the country was well on the way to modernisation on the western European pattern.

Turkey was still bureaucratically stultified and the people culturally and religiously restricted but it worked. It enthusiastically imported the best of western technology, provided an improving standard of living for its citizens and declined foreign adventures. It raised, educated and employed (although not fully) a growing population, which today has reached over 70 million – an exponential rate of growth. Turkey has created forestry reserves covering 26% of the country, 33 national parks and many smaller parks, protected (sometimes in principle only) the surviving ruins and sites, created museums and archaeological departments. It has spent far too much on the military, carved too many dams, mines, roads and airports out of the rural landscape and left far too little money for education and welfare.

Rural Turkey is now light years away from the cities – although the basic technologies of electricity, pumped water, the telephone and TV have long-since reached every village, decline has set in. The European Union policy of cutting farm support subsidies (a backbone of the Kemalist administrations), climate change caused by global warming and the centralising of the school and health systems is accelerating the drift from country to town. Until the 1970's about 30% of the population lived in towns; today about 30% live in the country.

Present day rural Turkey is inhabited by old people, poor farmers or minorities with little commitment to the land or optimism for the future; they are often neglected or exploited by the centralised authorities. Villages are surrounded by forestry land on which villagers have no rights, governed by an officious burocracy and served by an inadequate social infrastructure. They are also, paradoxically, set in the heart of the most satisfying, relaxing and comforting place on earth.

If you have read the chapter on the history of Pamphylia and Pisidia, the next question is how to identify remains and to fit them into the historical context.

So far, in our area, evidence of Hittite occupation is limited to sites at Eflatunpınar on the east side of Beyşehir Lake, and at Kusura, near Dinar, the capital of the Hittite kingdom prior to the relocation to Hattusas, near Ankara, in the 16th century BC. We know that the Hittite name for the area was Pitassa and some *höyüks* have surface traces of pottery from this period. Few have been excavated, so substantial Hittite or Phrygian artefacts may lie undiscovered.

The Greek presence was confined mainly to Pamphylia, where the cities of Perge, Sillyon and Aspendos were early foundations, dating as far back as the 2nd millennium. Subsequently, these ancient sites were built over, so evidence of Greek occupation is obscured by Roman constructions. Pisidian cities, often with obscure origins, were re-established during or after Augustus' time and the main ruins date from the 1st and 2nd centuries, with rebuilding and addition of monasteries and churches until the 6th or 7th century, when Muslim incursions and raids effectively prevented the building of anything except fortifications.

Architectural history starts again with the Selçuks, who established settlements sometimes on totally new sites, sometimes on old, with a new and efficient road system to support trade across the country. The Ottomans continued the Selçuk tradition of building for trade, as well as for the state and religion.

Private house styles developed according to local weather conditions and building materials - in our area, limestone and timber are plentiful and are used as traditional materials. In coastal areas, traditional houses have an overhanging timber upper floor which catches the breeze; inland, all-stone buildings are more common. Roofs are usually of pan-tiles, but in mountain areas chestnut slats were once common. Traditional buildings are rapidly giving way to modern concrete blocks - nearly all city housing is in flats and the villages are now adopting the same style. Present-day public building is usually in lumpy unimaginative concrete.

City layout

Depending on the period, their size and wealth, Roman cities had similar layouts and public buildings, determined by the main roads and the water supply. Roads often crossed in the city centre, were decorated with commemorative arches at the point where they entered the city and were lined with graves / *necropolis* outside the city walls. Aqueducts conducted water for several kilometres from a source of the required purity and height and, entering the city on arches, delivered the water to the richest houses, the public baths and fountains. These build-ings had to be sited where they could be gravity-fed with water, so are often in the lowest part of the city. At the city centre was a market place / *agora* with pillared arcades of shops, temples and a council chamber / *bouleterion* for the town elders. A *gymnasium* complex (both school and sports hall) included baths and so was often built on lower ground. Outside the city, often built into a convenient hillside, was the theatre. If there was a racetrack / *stadium*, that would also be built on level ground outside the city.

After 312, when Christianity became legal, churches were converted from older buildings and later monasteries were established outside the cities. Selçuk and Ottoman towns included a similar range of buildings, often endowed by the rulers or upper classes. These included mosques complexes with religious schools / *medrese*, hospitals and shops, public baths / *ham-am*, covered markets / *bedestan* or *han* devoted to specific trades, and official buildings like the governor's house and law courts. Some towns were fortified with a castle and surrounded by re-built Roman walls; most were divided into different quarters according to the religious affiliations of the residents.

Outside the cities, Roman and Selçuk roads and bridges are quite distinct - main Roman roads were designed for wheeled traffic; Selçuk ones were made for mule, donkey or camel caravans. The Selçuks and Ottomans also built *kervansarays* on their main highways.

Below is a brief guide to the main points of Roman and Selçuk / Ottoman building style:

Walls

Even though nearly all the surviving buildings are of local limestone, there were several significant changes to building methods and styles.

The Greeks used massive rectangular stone blocks in a 'cushion' shape, laid in courses which bulge out along their length. The Romans used rectangular or sometimes hexagonal blocks but these tended to be smaller and without the rounded face. Late Roman walls, when the cities were rebuilt after earthquakes or re-fortified in face of raids, usually consist of hastily built mixtures of slabs and rubble, often with re-used stones incorporated into them. Byzantine and later walls often contain a large amount of brick and rubble, usually with courses of dark-red tiles at intervals. The Selçuks sometimes re-built existing walls, often incorporating earlier inscribed or decorated stones, which may be laid anyhow, regardless of the decoration. After this time cities were not fortified, as the land was under united rule, although some fortresses and many *kervansarays* were built of smooth, dressed stone.

Arches, Vaults and Domes

Doorways and means of supporting roofs differ according to period. Greek buildings almost never incorporated an arch, but used massive uprights and lintels. Roofs were made of wood and rooms could only be as wide as the length of available trees. The arch was introduced by the Romans from about 40 BC and not only enabled doorways to be wider, but also led to the construction of arched or vaulted stone roofs. Instead of being built on a stone platform foundation, buildings on sloping ground could be supported by arched vaults; in theatres, tiers of seats could be supported by arched passageways instead of being built into a hillside. Bridge building in stone became possible.

In late Roman times, the technique of supporting a dome on a square by means of corner squinches was perfected. Byzantine church building developed from the Roman basilica, and took the form either of three parallel aisles, with columns taking the weight of the raised central roof, or of a dome over the centre of a cross-shaped ground plan (dome over transept). The dome was often supported by arches rising from four great pillars. As buildings became more complicated, Byzantine architects used brick on upper stories, as it is lighter than stone.

Later on, the Selçuk Turks carried the use of the arch, often pointed, with a keystone and carefully keyed blocks in the arch, to fantastic lengths. In particular, the doors of public buildings were given great prominence and topped by enormously high decorated arches, with beautifully carved strip decoration around the arch and niches each side of the door. In many *kervansarays*, all internal walls are arched for lightness. Like the Byzantines, the Selçuks used brick domes but the bricks were often laid in herringbone patterns with blue-glazed tiles fitted into the pattern.

Ottoman buildings incorporated lower, round-topped arches, and the profile of a classic Ottoman mosque is a series of small domes surrounding one raised central dome. Baths have rows of domes pierced by glass lighting ducts.

Decoration

The earliest type of column capital, the Doric, is not seen in our area. The Ionic capital, first seen about 600 BC, has pairs of scrolls and was followed later by the Corinthian, which has acanthus leaves. The Romans used Ionian and Corinthian columns on different stories of the same building. They also used alternately arched and triangular pediments over recesses for statues, for example on theatre stages. Typical decoration on friezes in public buildings included swags of foliage with heads of Eros, Nike, Medusa or bull heads representing Zeus. Roman portraiture includes many statues of military leaders or emperors, dressed in their distinctive army uniform with decorated breastplate. Late Roman tombstones often have very rigid and formal portraits of the deceased, sometimes with their family, either reclining on banqueting couches or standing in military uniform. Very late figure carving (3rd century on) has the perspective-less look of Byzantine art, and faces often have very crudely executed staring eyes. Gradually the drill replaced the chisel as the tool for making friezes - unfinished pieces show clearly how they were made.

Selçuk and Beylik architectural decoration is very distinctive; it often incorporates formal Arabic script, bands of chisel-cut motifs interspersed with mouldings, and use of *muquarnas* (a honeycomb pendentive decoration). Interior painting is often stunning; timber roofs were decorated in blues, reds and golds with formal flower motifs along the beams. The other great innovation was the decorated and glazed tile, often in multi-sided shapes, sometimes bearing Arabic script, flower or even animal and human paintings. Initially the colours were dull greens and browns, but soon a vivid turquoise blue came into use and tiles were used for exterior decorations, around doorways, on minarets and on tombs.

Ottoman mosques are often of simple dressed stone, initially decorated in green tiles. Later İznik decorated tiles usually have a plain white ground with flower designs in deep blue, turquoise and a beautiful soft red. Wall decoration made lavish use of calligraphy, sometimes painted directly onto the walls, especially as medallions set on the squinches or dome supports, otherwise as framed illustrations.

Inscription styles

Three main scripts are found in Pamphylia and Pisidia – Greek, the native language of the country from before Hellenistic times to the 13th century and beyond, Latin, the 'official' language in the *coloniae* founded by Augustus and his successors, and Arabic, used for quotations from the Koran or dedications on Selçuk and Ottoman buildings. Turkish was written in Arabic script until 1925. Latin inscriptions are uncommon; early Arabic ones are more rigid and formal than later ones.

The age of Greek inscriptions can be ascertained by the way certain characters are written. In particular, the A written with a downward-pointing crossbar and omega written as a rounded W were introduced in about 40 BC. Dedicatory inscriptions in Latin can be seen on anything from triumphal arches to tombstones; Antioch has many examples. The most magnificent examples of Selçuk Arabic script framed the doors of the mosques, *medreses* / religious schools and *kervansarays* that adorned their roads and towns. Calligraphy had become an elegant, flowing art form (in Islam, depiction of the human form is forbidden and representative art discouraged). In Ottoman times calligraphy was mostly practiced either in metalwork or in painted form, and has survived mainly inside mosques. Arabic numerals were used until after 1923; as was the Hijri dating system (ie. 622AD of the Julian calendar is year zero, incremented by 12 lunar months for each year, so that the date of New Year moves forward by 10 days for each Julian calendar year.) It's strange to see a gravestone with someone born in (say) 1423 dying in (say) 1936.

Religious monuments

Early temples were built with a *peristyle* (rows of massive, fluted columns) surrounding an inner sanctuary and topped by a triangular *pediment* fronting a tiled roof. Roman temples were lighter and more ornate, with more marble, granite columns and less massive blocks in the walls. The *peristyle* was often omitted and the temple side-walls extended forward to support the roof and pediment with a few columns, with Ionic or Corinthian capitals, across the front.

In 385 AD Christianity became the official religion of the Empire and the first churches were constructed, re-using sites and stones of older buildings. Early churches are of the basilica type - a nave and side naves, divided by columns, with a rounded apse at the east end. The altar was situated in the apse, which had a hidden passage behind it for the priests to exit or enter at appropriate moments. The stonework is often rough and has rubble cores; it was plastered over and decorated with frescos. Later churches were often of dome over transept construction, with arched roofs over the arms of the cross and the dome supported on massive pillars.

Churches were sometimes converted into mosques by the closing up of the apse and addition of a *minaret* and a prayer niche / *mihrab* oriented to Mecca. Purpose-built Selçuk mosques were either rectangular in plan or adapted to fit the site. Often mosques were part of a complex including a founder's *turbe* / tomb, a *medrese* and maybe a hospital or poorhouse. Initially, many were built with timber roofs supported by huge timber columns; some re-used existing Roman columns, complete with capitals. The timber used was long-lasting cedar or juniper, both virtually insect-proof. Where timber was not available, Selçuk architects used domed brick roofs, with the bricks often laid in herringbone patterns and sometimes embedded with turquoise tiles.

The plan of an Ottoman mosque was usually square, with a *mihrab* on the east side and entrance on the west; entry was into an attached courtyard with an ablutions fountain and a porch around the entrance door. *Minarets* were awarded according to the status of the mosque; mosques with six *minarets* were reserved for the caliph and in rural areas one was considered sufficient. Modern mosques, although generally built of concrete, use the same plan.

Funeral Monuments

The most important type of grave, the free-standing temple tomb, had a temple facade with sometimes two Ionic columns and a portico with entrance door leading to a grave chamber where the dead were laid on benches. From the columns and style of the stonework, we know these are from the late Hellenistic or Roman period. In addition there are many simple graves, sometimes cut from solid rock, and usually more difficult to date. These include:

> Sargophagus tombs – a grave cut from a stone block with a pitched fitted lid
>
> Chamosorion tomb – a pitched lid over a grave chamber cut from bed-rock
>
> Vaulted roofed tombs – a later variant of the temple tomb

Selçuk *türbe* were often cylindrical or hexagonal stone constructions, topped by a pointed stone roof. They are rare in this area but common further east. Less important people were buried in graves marked by head and footstones crowned with a symbol of their rank, often a turban shape; Ottomans used the same grave styles. In mountainous areas people were often buried on a pass or viewpoint in a simple wooden-framed grave.

Along the route you may see headstones with distinctive patterns made of lines of holes punched into a flat slab. There is no evidence of an inscription. They're sometimes associated with mosques, sometimes alone. We've been unable to discover more about these graves, although there's a local tradition that they belong to Hungarian soldiers who settled here in Ottoman times.

Roads, bridges and *kervansarays*

This whole area is full of examples of wonderful antique roads. While they continued in use for centuries and therefore are often impossible to date with any sort of accuracy, there are some pointers. First, Roman roads were often initially military constructions and ran as far as possible directly between garrison towns. They were designed for marching men to walk abreast and the main ones carried wheeled vehicles, so are wide enough for a cart. They were ditched on either side and, at least near frontiers, the undergrowth was cleared for some distance on each side to deter ambushes. In general, they avoided flat valley bottoms, which might be marshy, and ran on raised ground at the base of the hills, or on an embankment. They climbed hills via broad bends or long diagonal slopes rather than at a steep gradient. Building materials varied according to local conditions, but normally they were edged with kerb stones and filled in with smaller stones. In areas where easily-shaped limestone slabs were available, they could be built of huge slabs laid right across the width of the road. Bridges were wide enough for a cart and edged with a parapet; they might have a single arch or many arches built on buttresses set in a river-bed.

Later Selçuk, Beylik or Ottoman roads were trade routes built for mule or camel traffic and could be narrower and with steeper gradients. They are often beautifully cobbled *kaldırım*, writhing along hillsides, with a stone parapet on the lower side. Bridges were narrower, of single or multiple pointed arches of great elegance.

Kervansarays, spaced one day's march apart, were high-walled, easily-defended rectangular buildings with only one exterior door. Inside was a great hall and accommodation for men and their animals around a courtyard; kitchens, store-rooms, a *hamam* and a *mescit /* small mosque completed the facilities.

Private houses

There are no excavated villas in Pamphylia or Pisidia. Many of the older and more remote villages in this region, however, have retained houses built in a traditional, vernacular style which has remain unchanged since the middle ages. Most of these houses are a mixture of stone (or occasionally brick) and timber, materials locally available and which provide the best combination of winter warmth and coolness in the heat of summer. The timber laid between courses of stone in the walls is to absorb the shock of earth tremors. Pitched, tiled roofs are the norm, as they repel winter rains and are cooler in summer than flat roofs.

The ground floor of these houses was devoted to livestock and storage, though this practice is on the wane. The main focus of the living quarters is the *selamlık* or *baş oda*, a reception room used for the (male) head of the household to entertain villagers and travellers. This is the room in which you, as a traveller through the region, will receive hospitality. Seating here is usually in the form of raised divans or beds lining the walls, covered in hand-embroidered throws and cushions. Some older houses still retain wooden fireplaces, but most villagers have now installed basic wood-burning stoves. Unfortunately many of the older village houses are badly neglected, with the younger generation preferring houses with a reinforced concrete frame, infilled with cheap, hollow clay bricks skimmed with cement.

Using the above clues, you can estimate the period and age of ruins or buildings encountered, even if they are not listed in any of the guidebooks. You will very quickly recognise the different architectural styles, and feel sympathy for the people who lived dignified and simple lives in the countryside. One of the benefits of walking is that you have time to work out why towns and roads were sited as they were, what crops could have been grown, and so on.

If you are specifically walking for the historical context of the route, then the most interesting areas are the Graeco-Roman sites at Perge, Pednelissos, Adada, Aspendos, Selge and Antioch in Pisidia, Selçuk period sites at Sütçüler, Eğirdir and Yalvaç and the village houses of Sütçüler, Barla, Eyüpler, Sücüllü and Yalvaç. The most interesting roads are the Roman roads at Çandır – Sütçüler, Müezzinler – Adada and around Selge, and the later Selçuk roads around Çimenova – Çukurca – Kesme, near Serpil, and Yukarı Tırtar – Eyüpler (Pazar Yolu).

If you find anything unusual, for example, if you notice an inscription on a re-used stone in a house wall, or find an isolated ruin, take a photo or copy the inscription, and make a note of exactly where you saw it. We shall be very pleased to hear from you and will forward interesting information to a museum.

6 NATIONAL PARKS, FLORA & FAUNA

Before describing the environments en route, it's appropriate to note that much of the land around the route in the Taurus mountains is owned by the Forestry and Environment Ministry. Turkey's forests are owned and managed by this Ministry, which is charged with producing timber products, managing erosion and re-forestation zones and water resources, creation and management of National and Forest park and other recreational facilities and developing a co-operative relationship inside their boundaries allowing income generation for villagers living in forestry villages. Turkey's forests were only nationalised in 1945, and the Ministry in its final form not developed until the 1960's, so the progress made in this area covers a very short time span. The Forestry Ministry owns some 26% of the land area of Turkey; only just over 50% of this is productive forest, the rest is made up of erosion areas, plantations, national parks, areas above the tree-line, etc.

State forests are managed to produce Turkey's timber needs; this is not completely success-ful as the timber produced is often not of particularly high quality and more and more timber is being imported. But the forests are well managed in that they are very rarely clean cut; timber is allowed to regenerate naturally and mixed undergrowth flourishes. Unsurfaced forest roads are driven through to permit management, but most become overgrown again after a cut has been completed. This creates a lovely environment for walking, mountainbiking and camping, activities permitted in most forests.

The National and Forest Parks are usually designed to protect a specific habitat, such as forests of particular endemic species, but to date not much attention has been paid to the biodiversity in these areas. However, the Forestry Ministry ran a pilot project (GEF II) in four National Parks to measure the biodiversity, take steps to preserve it and develop management plans. The plans have been delayed, but they have highlighted sustainable tourism, a new ven-ture for both the Forestry engineers and the villagers. Because of this, the Ministry co-operated on the creation of this long distance route.

The specific National and Forest Parks en route are the Kurşunlu Waterfalls, Yazılı Canyon, Köprülü Canyon, Tota Yaylası, Kovada Lake and Kasnak Forest. The Culture and Tourism Ministry also issues preservation orders on specific natural features, for example the centuries-old plane trees in Barla village, as well as historic sites.

The area of the route is limestone, folded and raised to form the Taurus mountains with, to the north, the level plateau of central Turkey. Because all the runoff from the central plateau enters the sea via rivers flowing through the Taurus, many of the river valleys have become eroded canyons of vast depth. They are in places too steep-sided to allow modern roadways to pass, so north-south routes are limited and east-west routes almost non-existent. The main north-south route is a natural corridor via passes north of Antalya. Along the Asku river and through the Çandir Canyon, a Roman road formed a north-south route; this was in use until maybe the 1950's. It was lost when the bridges fell in an earthquake; later part of the route was drowned under the Karacaören dam lake. The construction of this dam resulted in loss of agricultural land and trade income to the Sütçüler/Çandır area.

Similarly, Roman roads along the Köprülü Canyon were once used during the annual mi-gration of flocks of goats from the coast to the mountain plateaux between Lakes Eğirdir and Beyşehir. Since the main migration stopped, old roads in the Köprülü canyon have fallen into disuse and been replaced by a new asphalt road on the opposite bank. The area to the north of both canyons is now isolated, especially in winter, by poor roads over difficult terrain. This isolation adds to the charm of the route and has enabled nature to flourish, but has made it difficult for farmers to bring crops to market.

The area of the route covers rapid changes of altitude and climate and the environment varies from deep forest to steppe, so it's impossible to generalise about the wildlife. In the route section there are specific notes about each of the National or Forest parks which the route crosses. Below are some brief notes about the types of habitat on and around the route.

Wetlands

Turkish wetlands are under threat from dams, drainage for agriculture and climate change. The only surviving wetlands directly on this route are around Lakes Eğirdir and Kovada and areas near Çandır and Kemerdamları. Pinched between agricultural areas and poisoned by chemical runoff, they are still a valuable habitat for birds and marsh orchids. Lakeside trees include huge *çınar* and willows. The meadows are filled with buttercups, bellevalia, marsh orchids, summer snowflake and irises, the water edges with reeds and willows, sometimes extending far out into the lake. Eğirdir lake itself once had a huge population of over-wintering ducks; hunting has decimated them. The artificial southern lakes, Kovada and Karacaören, have varying water levels so their bird populations are much lower. May and June are good times for bird-watching around the lakes, and my favourite site is Kemerdamları, where a strip of damp meadows and marshes border the lake. The most spectacular water birds are herons (grey, purple, night and squacco), storks, spoonbills, marsh harriers and ruddy shelducks but grebes, little bittern, wagtails, kingfishers, reed warblers, terns and shrikes are also associated with the damp habitat. Rarities are black storks and glossy ibis.

Scrub

The typical Mediterranean low scrub of kermes oak, Jerusalem sage, cistus and broom, covers many areas at lower altitudes. Where the scrub has been able to mature a little, carob trees, wild olives, wild pistachio and bay tree spring up. Above the kermes oak scrub, from about 1200m, in areas where mature trees have been cut and grazing animals prevents regrowth, juniper scrub is scattered across the mountain sides; cyclamen, colchicum and autumn crocus flower here. Areas on Davraz and Barla are under particular pressure from over-grazing.

If you can find an area where the goats have been held at bay, wild flowers, especially spring flowering bulbs, range from anemones to muscari, tulips and iris. Helleborine, various ophrys and other orchids are often present. Scrub birds at all levels include many warblers; olivaceous, olivetree, Ruppel's, blackcap, lesser whitethroat and Bonelli's; various wheatears, rufous bush robin, white-throated robin, serin and red-fronted serin, ortolan and Cretzchmar's bunting and the ubiquitous black-headed bunting. The loud, deep scold of yellow-vented bulbul is heard near the coast and the explosive call of Cetti's warbler in taller scrub near water. Buzzards, usually long-legged buzzards, are common birds of prey.

Forest

The forest is clearly defined by altitude – cedar only grows naturally above about 1500m up to the tree-line at about 1800m; juniper grows mixed with and below the cedar; pines are usually at lower levels still. Two types of pine grow here; the black pine and *pinus brutia* - easy to spot because it has redder bark and bears far more cones. The forests are rarely pure pine; *arbutus*, carob, the Judas tree, styrax and myrtle are usually mixed in wherever light permits. Where the soil is deeper, oaks, including the local endemic volcanic oak, replace the pines. The most beautiful tree is undoubtedly the cedar, sometimes growing to great size, with tactile, smooth cones held up like candles. There are large junipers and larch around the Köprülü valley, especially just below Selge, and spruce and Scots pine on the hills above Çaltepe. All along the watercourses grow deciduous *çınar*, some of monumental size.

Flower growth depends on the amount of light, so most flowers grow on the outskirts of the forest or in clearings. After tree-felling, the disturbance to the soil and the exposure to light allows a crop of orchids (mainly Anatolian, pinewood and dactylorhiza species) to spring up. Cyclamen, *sternbergia*, and *fritillaria* also flourish, with star of Bethlehem, grape hyacinth, especially the large *muscari comosum*, iris and *peony maculata* in clearings. Snowdrops and primroses grow by stream-beds at higher elevations.

Most obvious forest birds are the tits, including sombre tit and long tailed tit, the nut-hatches, especially Kreuper's, and the finches; chaffinch, greenfinch and occasionally crossbills. Woodpeckers are common in mixed forest and three or four varieties can sometimes be observed together. Redstarts and wrens are common in mature open forest.

Steppe

For centuries, the central plateau has been deforested and used for agriculture, but between the fields are a few scattered trees, often pears or hawthorns. Poplars, planted for a quick timber crop, have been reintroduced and willows grow along the streams. Plants include wild gladioli, flaxes in yellow and blue, asphodelines and arums. Around Yalvaç, flowering in May is a low-growing brilliant red saphrophytic plant called *phelypaea coccinea*.

Birds are obvious in this environment and flock birds are easy to spot. The most beautiful are the bee-eaters, which nest in colonies near Yalvaç, but swallows and swifts are also common near water or suitable nest sites. Goldfinch favour thistle patches, orioles the poplar trees, Isabelline wheatears and larks the ground, cuckoos the willows, rollers the telegraph wires and storks the telegraph poles. Flocks of Spanish sparrows nest below the storks and occasionally there are hedge sparrows – in hedges. Rarities are the greater spotted cuckoo, red-footed falcon, rock sparrow (higher up) and travelling flocks of rose-coloured starlings.

Mountains and canyons

The route ranges up to the treeline at 1800m and the nearby peaks up to 2799m (Barla), giving you the opportunity to spot many flowers and birds. The peaks are limestone, so water dissolves the rock and forms underground streams. Eventually the roofs collapse and result in hollows where earth collects; below the tree-line these hollows are usually filled with trees, but above they hold snow and damp soil when all around is dry. Only seasonal bulbs and small shrubs, usually prickly survivors, thrive above the treeline. At snowmelt, snow margins are covered with tiny miniatures; yellow *gagea*, bright blue *scilla* and an almost invisible brown fritillary are the most common. They are succeeded by *ornithogallum*, grape hyacinth of various dwarf varieties, more fritillaries and vast swathes of pink *colchicum* or the golden *crocus chrysanthus*.

The largest bird you are likely to see is the lammergeier, but golden and lesser-spotted eagles and Egyptian vultures are also around. The large black flock bird is the alpine chough; the small black and white one is the snowfinch, often seen with the horned shore lark. Around the tree-line you may see or hear chukar, a game-bird, and a little higher you may see the crimson-winged finch and Finsch's wheatear, the most handsome of birds in a black and white dinner jacket. Rock thrushes, blue rock thrushes and hoopoe also inhabit this zone.

The brown fish owl has been reported nesting in the canyons; this is the furthest west site where they have been recorded. Griffon vulture colonies amd wallcreeper are also found here.

Flowers

Please don't collect specimens, not even single flower-heads or seeds. The locals collect many of the orchids for *salep* (for making ice cream); commercial collectors pay for snowdrop bulbs or crocus corms and crazy collectors have uprooted rare orchids. If you need to identify something rare, take a photo and note the characteristics, place and date, but don't pass the location on to any amateur you don't know. If you are a botanist (amateur or professional) and would like to compile plant lists (especially bulbs) for different locations on the route for the

Forestry Ministry and for adding to the web site and i-phone app, please contact us. Some are already available on request.

Bird-watching

To identify the birds listed above, you will need binoculars and a bird guide. As in Europe, early mornings are good, except for the raptors, which are best after 11am. From midday to about 4 o'clock, small birds often rest. If you camp close to a water-source, it's worth checking which birds have come down to drink before you get out of your tent. If you systematically record your observations, we would be pleased to hear from you, especially if you have seen any of the real rarities.

Animals

Hunting has denuded Turkey of its larger mammals; some, such as wild goats, deer, lynx, wild cat, brown bear and wolf are protected; the lynx may, like the Anatolian leopard, be extinct. Many older shepherds remember their flocks being attacked by wolves and may still carry guns. The largest animal still flourishing is the wild pig, which is common in forest and near farms. Hunting is forbidden in the National Parks and in forest but the rules are frequently broken.

The animals you are most likely to see are smaller ones; foxes, Persian squirrels, badgers and marten. There is a wide variety of sun-loving creatures; snakes, lizards, tortoises and butterflies.

Seasons

Spring (April – May) is the best time for flowers, depending on altitude, and May is good for the bird migration and for hearing the calls. The migration brings all sorts of birds of passage, especially warblers. Butterflies are better a little later, in June and July. Autumn brings a fresh crop of flowers (and mushrooms) and the seasonal colouring of the forests, as well as the return migration, which reaches its peak in early October. In winter, flocks of ducks and grebe appear and mammals can be tracked from their prints in the snow.

This is not a comprehensive description, but just a taste of what you might find if you are prepared to carry binoculars and a flower or bird book.

Note that the route crosses the Aksu river at a concrete dam / regulatör. This is the only crossing place between the main coastal road and a road bridge many km upstream and is close to the ford at Çatallar (now under a dam) which St Paul must have used. From April-May to November this dam is easily passable; in winter the water is too fast and deep so you should start the route at the end of this stage, Akçapınar, which is accessible directly from Antalya; see section 7.3.

According to legend, after the fall of Troy in about 1200BCE, seven heroes, Mopsos, Calchas, Riksos, Labos, Machaon, Leonteus and Minyasas, travelled south from the battlefields and founded **Perge**. Positioned on the end of a ridge, close to the Kestros / Aksu river and about 12km from the open sea, Perge was protection from naval attack but could trade by sea. An outpost at the mouth of the river protected the city; some goods were offloaded there and brought to Perge on smaller ships. There is now no trace of a bridge or harbour on the river Kestros, presumably they were swept away by the frequent floods.

Perge was captured from the land by first the Persians then by Alexander the Great; it appears that there were no defensive walls at that time. After Alexander, while the Seleucid dynasty reigned, the city flourished in peace and prosperity. After 188BCE, the Romans passed Pamphylia to the Attalid kings of Pergamon. In 133BCE, when the Attalids died out, the Romans installed a governor, Manlius Aquillius, who rebuilt the main road from Perge to the interior via the Döşeme pass. Perge later shared its trade with the newly-founded Attaleia / Antalya, which had a better harbour.

Perge's temple to Diana / Artemis, famous for its size and its gold-clad statue of Diana, made it a major religious centre. The goddess was represented on some of Perge's coins, sometimes dressed as a huntress; other coins show the temple, which has yet to be found.

Under the Empire, the city grew into one of the most beautiful in all of Anatolia. New buildings included a *palaestra* dedicated to the Emperor Claudius and others, including the baths, *nymphaeum* and entrance complex, commissioned by a woman, Plancia Magna. This powerful woman was a high priest of the Artemis cult, head priestess of the Imperial cult, and the chief civil representative of the city. She came from a rich family which probably originated in Italy but which in the 2nd century owned extensive lands in Pisidia and Galatea. Her father was a Governor of Bythinia, her brother an athlete and she was related to Varus, the philosopher, who was known, from his long nose, as 'the stork'. Her portrait statue in Antalya museum shows her partly veiled and her tomb is in a prominent position outside the walls.

In the reign of Aurelian (270-75), Perge inaugurated a new series of sacred games, confirming its place as a leading city in state and religious affairs. An auxilliary legion, Cohors 1 Flavia Numidarum, was permanently stationed here to defend the area against attack from the sea. Perge later became an important centre of Christian worship with its own bishop.

The earthquakes and tidal waves of 530 and of 541 and the following plagues caused the citizens to abandon the lower city and retreat to the *acropolis*. The latest pottery is of the 7th century; around that time Arab raids finished off the city. In 754, the last known Bishop Sissinius (or Pastillas) of Perge is recorded as attending an Ecumenical Council, but he may have been resident in nearby Sillyon.

For nearly a thousand years, the site was almost undisturbed but, in 1743, an earthquake caused more buildings to fall. In 1911, after another quake, locals removed much stone to rebuild their village.

According to the Bible, in 46AD Paul, with Barnabas and Timothy, took ship from Cyprus and sailed to Perge, staying for a while before they continued to Antioch in Pisidia. On their return to Perge, Paul delivered a sermon before going to Antalya to take ship again.

Exploring Perge

Approaching Perge along the road from Aksu, on the left, built into the southern slopes of Kocabelen hill, is the theatre, fenced off as it is in dangerous condition. The cavea, slightly more than a semicircle, is divided in two by a wide gallery / *diazoma*, with 19 rows of seats below and 23 above, giving a capacity of 13,000 people. During the 3rd century, carved balustrades were erected around the orchestra in order to contain wild animals. The frieze on the two-storey stage building is now in Antalya Museum; it portrays the god of the Kestros river and Dionysos, god of wine and founder and protector of theatres. Another theatre frieze in the museum shows the goddess Tyche with worshippers and sacrificial bulls.

Right of the road is a well-preserved stadium measuring 34 x 334m, with seating for 12,000 people. It was built over 70 vaulted chambers, some forming entrances to the stadium, others used as shops.

Perge's first walls were built in the Hellenistic period but the current walls, which have low towers, were built in the 4th - 5th century against the threat of Isaurian bandits. The main entrance gate is flanked by a pair of Hellenistic cylindrical towers, once part of the original city walls and later modified by Plancia Magna. The gate leads to a courtyard where the walls, covered with marble slabs and decorated with niches and Corinthian columns, provided a background for nine statues of gods and goddesses. Above was a second tier of statues of the mythical city founders. On an arched gateway beyond the towers were statues of the Emperors with their wives.

Passing through the second gate, on the left is a public fountain / *nymphaeum* dedicated to Artemis and the emperor Septimius Severus, with a richly decorated two-storeyed façade and pool in front. North of this is the entrance to the most beautiful baths in Asia Minor; next to an exercise yard / *palaestra* is a pool once surrounded by statues set in coloured marble surrounds. Beyond is the cold pool / *frigidarium*, a second exercise area, the warm pool / *tepidarium* and the hot pool / *caldarium*. The warm pools are interconnected and built over a *hypocaust* system that circulated hot air from the boiler room.

On the right of the gate is an *agora*, surrounded by a wide, columned gallery / *stoa*, lined with shops once paved with coloured mosaics and with a circular water tower in the centre. Both here and along the main street, several columns have recently been re-erected.

The main street, which was cooled by a channel with flowing water and lined by columned *stoas* and shops, rises slightly up the hill, passing under another arch towards another *nymphaeum*, just below the *acropolis*. A road to the left leads to some early Byzantine churches and a bishop's palace. The cathedral church is a frescoed *basilica* with short transept arms and was built out of large limestone blocks; nearby is a five-aisled *basilica* with an entrance porch / *narthex* and couryard / *atrium*. Also close by is what may be a *triconchos* church (with the apse in clover leaf shape) and, beyond, another church incorporates re-used Doric columns. Rejoining the main street, near the *acropolis* a cross street leads left to a large exercise yard / *palaestra* and more baths built against the western city walls. On the *acropolis* are finds that go back to the 7th century BCE and the remains of churches of the 5th and 6th century, maybe part of a monastery complex.

The city has been under excavation since 1946 but only about 25% of the area has been uncovered. Recent excavations have unearthed many more sculptures, indicating that Perge had a major workshop carrying out final processing on marble figures and tombs. When you've finished your tour, leave the city via the main gate and turn north up the asphalt road.

Perge aqueduct delivered water from the Kurşunlu river to the *acropolis* hill. From there it was distributed to the city, including to the statue of the river god at the head of the water channel down the main street. From its start point at Kurşunlu waterfalls, the aqueduct closely followed the course of the Kurşunlu river for several km, then contoured a hill, crossed two valleys and approached the site on higher ground. It must have crossed the level land below the *acropolis* hill via a siphon. Low walls, calcified water deposits and two arched bridges over the valleys are visible along the route.

Perge - Kurşunlu (3hrs)

This route follows the Perge aqueduct to its source at a waterfall inside the Kurşunlu Nature Park, passing two bridges where the aqueduct crossed side-streams. Apart from the valley-crossings, the route is mostly nearly level and is partly on farm track and partly on path through forest. In places it's overgrown and you may have to make detours to avoid scrub.

From the road at the site, turn R/N and walk on the asphalt to a few large stone blocks near a greenhouse. Turn L onto dirt road; at a fork keep R and at the end of the road climb through an orchard towards the hillside. At the base of the hill, turn R and head towards a greenhouse. Just past this, find a path which climbs diagonally up the hillside, following the line of the aqueduct. From the hilltop, you have good views of Perge *acropolis* hill and the place where the aqueduct (presumably in a siphon) climbed to the top.

1hr

On the hilltop, continue through woodland above the cliff to a dirt road. Follow this for 200m then branch R onto lower ground. Descend steeply through scrub to the base of the first aqueduct over the valley beyond. Cross the stream-bed in the valley and find a path rising to an asphalt road.

30mins

Turn L then R onto a rising dirt track which curves L and begins to descend. Turn R onto footpath which approaches a deep valley; turn R along the valley and find the second aqueduct. Walk over it carefully, turn R and follow the line of the aqueduct through scrub on the far side of the valley. As the river bends R, leave it and climb to a large greenhouse - pass it on your R to a dirt road.

30mins

Turn R and follow the road past a second greenhouse, over a crossroads, past a small building to the edge of a wood. Here, bear L /NNW onto path and descend to cross a side-gully.

15mins

Continue NW, approaching the main river, finding slight traces of the aqueduct (lime, stalactites and old walls) alongside and above the Kurşunlu river as you approach the waterfalls. There is one more side-valley to cross, but there is no trace of an aqueduct here. Instead, there is an old road which climbs the far valley side to level ground. Here, the aqueduct presumably ran below on your R; walk through woodland towards the cluster of cafes close to the waterfalls. The park entrance/exit is 200m to your L /NW.

45mins

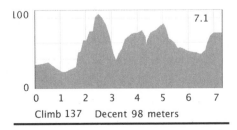

Climb 137   Decent 98 meters

Kurşunlu Nature Park was created in 1991 and enlarged later to give a total area of 586 hectares under protection. It is named after the Kurşunlu / lead falls and river. The water contains a high lead content and is coloured an unusual and spectacular, almost opaque, light green. The falls are about 15m high, curved in a bow shape, and have a rainbow above them when the sun is shining. Behind them are caves, accessible via the side of the falls. The river runs through low forest and maquis, mainly of pines, çınars, wild olives, the mastic tree and oleander scrub. The lower part of the river is bordered with reeds and full of water-lilies. The park provides a haven for wildlife, including ducks, moorhens and other water birds, many warblers, including the rare graceful warbler, wild pigs, martens, foxes and hares.

The park is so close to Antalya that it's a popular summer picnic spot; tourists also arrive by the coach-load. Swimming in the falls is forbidden, but that doesn't stop local daredevils from swinging on tree branches over the water, or splashing in the spray. There is a marked walk downstream parallel to the river, which leads to a fishing lodge; this area is almost deserted. Upstream and outside the park, on the next section of the walk, is a swimming place where the local children dive and splash.

The entrance is on the W side of the falls opposite a carpark; beyond here are a couple of restaurants but they're quite a walk from the park itself and mainly cater for tour groups. There's a small admission charge and the gates are locked at night. Inside the gates are shops and an expensive restaurant and café. If you have your own food, there are picnic tables around under the pine trees. There are fairly frequent buses to Antalya east bus station and a *dolmuş* services in summer. You could camp on the level ground on the E side of the falls, up the steps beyond the small toilet block.

140

20

0

Climb 172

KURŞUNLU – AKÇAPINAR 7.2

Kurşunlu – Akçapınar junction via the Regulatör (7hr 20mins)

This route follows the tarmac road for a few km then turns R onto forest track, following higher ground then descending towards the river. It crosses via the regulator and wanders through farmland to join a side-river. Akçapınar is 2km beyond. Most of the route is on easy track; see below for information about the regulatör.

Go out of the main gate of the forest park and turn R onto asphalt, heading NW then NE. Walk about 500m to the roadbridge; if you turn R here, there is a swimming place below the bridge; to the L are restaurants and a camping place. Continue on the main road, which runs NE between forests to a junction with a forest road on the R.

1hr

Turn R/SE onto forest road for 250m then L, crossing a junction to reach a T junction. Turn R/ENE and continue NNE on this road for 1km, crossing a junction with minor tracks. Approaching woodland, turn sharp L/NW.

30mins

After only 100m, turn R /NNE, descend to woodland and cross a stream-bed; climb the far side to a track. Walk N and where the paths divide keep R; continue with farmland below /R to a T junction.

35mins

Turn R and after 75m L /NNW with an orchard on your L. Continue through more woodland to reach a forest track; turn L and follow it NW to a T junction then E to a crossroads.

25mins

Turn L / N to a deep stream bed; on the far side, bear NW and find a rising track which continues N out of the forest, through a pretty mahalle to an asphalt road. There is an interesting well on the R.

30mins

Turn R onto asphalt for 500m then L onto forest track. Branch R and continue N between greenhouses and houses, then through forest to a second asphalt road.

30mins

Turn L/ENE for 500m then R onto forest track; after a km bear L then L again to a sharp bend where the track rises. Here, descend to the stream below, cross just above a waterfall and climb to the second track on the far side.

40mins

This wide track curves L, passes remains of an old mill then continues around a valley head then N or NE, climbing gently past several junctions and across a major track. After the wide track, take the 2nd L track going N; the houses of Gülölük are visible below/L.

45mins

Approaching the track end, turn L onto an old path, which descends with a gully on the R then continues more steeply downwards towards farmland. Just before the buildings turn R to a road, turn R again and L / downhill past the school to the main village road.

1hr 10mins

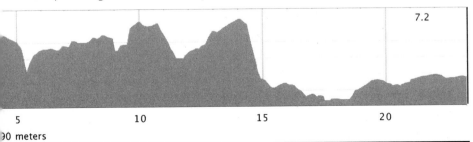

7.2

5   10   15   20

90 meters

	Turn L to the mosque; just before it, turn R and continue NE through greenhouses and farmland then through scrub and past more greenhouses to a junction. Turn R and walk downhill to cross the irrigation canal on a bridge. Turn L on crumbling asphalt and walk 200m to the gate of the park surrounding the regulator.
50mins	

Crossing the Regulatör

This crossing of the Aksu river is passable from April to the rainy season, normally November; locals use it regularly. The *regulatör* is enclosed in a small forest park and approached by a gated track lined with eucalyptus. If the gate is padlocked, bypass it through the bushes. Walk up the track to the massive concrete sluice gates flanking the stream. R is a concrete bulwark with a metal ladder leading down to the 400m-long concrete dam across the river. The route goes across the river on this 90cm wide dam-top; in late summer when the water is low, the top can be slippery with slime. Check the water depth before you cross; if it's below knee-depth then the crossing is ok. Below the dam is a belt of vegetation so even if you slip you are unlikely to get swept downstream, just into a bit of mud.

Re-pack your rucksack if necessary to ensure that all items are in waterproof bags. Roll up your trousers or change into shorts; remove your boots and tie them to your rucksack before descending the ladder. If you have sandals, cross in them; make sure your walking-poles (if you have them) are accessible. Leave your rucksack waist belt undone so you can slip it off easily if required. Cross the dam carefully, using the poles to support you on the concrete surface. At the far side is a similar ladder; there's also the regulatör keeper's house, a tap and picnic tables.

	From the river crossing, walk E down the road with a canal on the R to a junction by a bridge. Turn L/N and cross (or ford) the wide gravel bed of a tributary of the river; continue on track uphill towards the village of Akçay on the hill. From the start of the village, the road is asphalt; continue along the ridge, passing a *çeşme* opposite a graveyard to a T-junction on lower ground.
50mins	
	Turn R/E and 100m later R again; take the 2nd L turn onto a tractor track with a wooded bank on the L; follow the track around several bends to a T junction by a major irrigation canal. Turn L /N for 200m to a road and a bridge over the irrigation channel and stream.
45mins	
	The road ahead rises to Akçapınar on the hill ahead; the next section runs L/N and parallel with the river.

The sizeable village of **Akçapınar** occupies a long ridge hilltop site overlooking the Aksu valley. On the main square, below the mosque, there is a *bakkal* with a limited range of supplies and a *kahve*. In the lower part of the village are more shops and many old timber houses with overhanging balconies, decaying gently. There is a noisy ATV track outside the village.

Between November and April, we recommend that you join the route at Akçapınar. Take a bus from Antalya to the country town of Gebiz; from here a *dolmuş* runs to Akçapınar 3-4 times per day; get off the *dolmuş* at its final stop near a large mosque. The asphalt road to the route runs downhill/SW then W from the mosque, passing a track for ATV's, and meeting the route after 1km at the bridge.

Akçapınar - Uçansu 1 (2hrs 40 mins)

The route runs along the banks of the Uçansu river to the first of two towering waterfalls, Uçansu I, where it's possible to swim. All of the route is on track, in places crossing the river via shallow fords, which may be almost dry in summer/autumn. To save removing your boots, you could walk the whole route in sandals.

Follow the track with the river on your L, running due N. At first this is awkward because gravel has been extracted from the river-bed, but soon the track becomes clear and comfortable to walk on. It crosses to the W bank, re-crosses and then continues through woodland on the W of the stream. After a steady uphill walk, at a fork, choose the R branch and cross to the E bank, going NW. Where the track forks, choose the L branch and cross the river again to the W bank.

1hr 10mins

The track rises N, away from the river and cutting off a loop then approaching the river with fields on the R. Cross to the E bank to cut off a second loop, mainly through woodland but with fields and orchards. Cross again to the W bank and cross open fields; recross and at a junction with a main track turn L/N then to the L again, cutting off a loop of the river. A few minutes on, it switches to the L bank again and swings upwards and away from the river. After passing through hedges and cultivated fields, some with beehives, the track forks; take the R/downward fork and cross the stream to the R bank.

50mins

From here the track continues N then curves E in woodland, passing several junctions. At a final junction keep L; you will see the upper part of the waterfall as it plunges over the cliff ahead; beyond it is Bodrumkaya, the rocky outcrop above the site of Pednelissos. Keep L and walk the final 250m to the open area at the base of the falls.

40mins

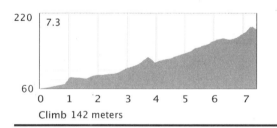

```
220  7.3


 60
     0   1   2   3   4   5   6   7
     Climb 142 meters
```

The **Uçansu 1** / flying falls, and the pool below them, are a spectacular and refreshing sight. The water plunges from a great height (perhaps 40m) over rocks coated with coloured lime deposits shaped into great hanging fans, into a 25m wide pool of unfathomable depth. The pool is surrounded by huge *çınar* with gnarled roots grabbing at the rocks and oleander bushes; the turquoise-tinted slightly opaque water is very tempting to a hot trekker. There is a *pınar* on the R side of the falls in a niche overgrown by ferns. Close by the falls, right over the water, is a timber-built restaurant; you could stay the night here, sleeping on their terrace. At weekends in summer, the falls are busy with picnickers and jeep-tour groups; in early spring there is unlikely to be anyone around.

Uçansu I falls - Hasgebe via Pednelissos (3hrs 50mins)

The route climbs past Uçansu I to Uçansu II, a similar but deserted waterfall. Above here, it follows the stream to the graveyard at Kozan, then on track and Roman road to the heart of the site of Pednelissos. It crosses the ridge of Bodrumkaya and descends to the village of Hasgebe. There is some track but most of the route is on footpath or Roman road. The views from the top of the falls and from the walls of Pednelissos are spectacular.

35mins | Retrace your steps for 100m to a L turn into woodland before the last junction. Climb SE then NE through pines, looking carefully for waymarks, passing the lower falls on your L and approaching a track on the R. Join the track and turn L/N. Walk on the track to Uçansu II waterfalls, crossing the stream just below the falls.

> The **Uçansu II** / flying falls, and the pool below them, are more isolated and overgrown with vegetation than Uçansu I. The falls are of similar height and the pool equally spectacular and inviting and the vegetation keeps the surroundings cool. There is no level ground space for camping by the falls, but an ideal place above them. Also on the stream above the falls are well-worn stone remains of an ancient mill building; it must have served the city of Pednelissos.

35mins | On the W side of the falls, walk W/upwards to pick up a track which bends R/NW and climbs through forest. Where it bends L/SW towards a clear ridge, turn R onto a well-used but narrow stony footpath which climbs through dense bushes to the top of the falls. As you approach the stream, you could turn R to the viewpoint at the top of the falls. The marked path continues NE to a grassy area on the W bank where you could camp.

10mins | Cross the narrow stream and turn L/N/parallel with it, crossing a *kanalet* and a field and approaching a cottage. Here, the path swings R/up to meet a dirt road.

15mins | Turn R and then L; cross a second road and climb between houses onto a footpath which soon decends through pines to meet a dirt road at a graveyard; turn L.

> This track winds 1.3km through woodland to a house, restaurant and small pension in a garden. Beyond here is the rest of **Kozan** village, a few scattered houses on the slopes of Bodrumkaya, the massive outcrop where Pednelissos is situated. Opposite the mosque, in the yard of the (empty) school are pieces of Corinthian column and traces of an old road. Kozan has no bus and no *bakkal.*

40mins | From Kozan, retrace your steps along the main dirt road to the graveyard. Turn E onto a wide track and a few hundred metres later turn L/NNE onto a path which crosses a track and climbs to the indistinct remains of a Roman road. Soon the slabs of the old road are clearly visible, climbing steeply through the trees. Approaching the edge of the forest, turn L/down onto a clear track then climb R over rough stone to meet a dirt track at a large pine.

10mins | Continue NNE/uphill on dirt road towards and through the site.

Continue on rising track to Bodrumkaya and bear L/NW along the rock face, following a footpath to some huge cisterns. Past them, the track forks - R is a final cistern with a crenellated stone beam over it. Turn R on the Roman road which runs N, through a gap in the ridge of Bodrumkaya then descends in bends through woodland. It crosses an open area then follows a winding dirt track to the stream at the bottom of the valley; just beyond is the narrow asphalt road.

1hr 10mins

Turn R and follow the road downhill; the Roman road is in the bushes on the L. Just after a small waterfall, at the start of Hasgebe, a dirt road branches L/NE; the route continues on this.

15mins

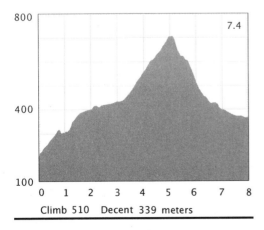

Climb 510   Decent 339 meters

From Hellenistic times or even before, Pednelissos was a well developed and defended city with all the amenities of civilisation. Although the site was in a position ideal for defence, it also commanded a trade corridor up the Kestros river and was an early religious centre possibly allied with Side.

As you approach the city, to the right is a section of the upper city walls, which enclosed an *acropolis* or defensive area; there were more city walls below these; turn R off the track towards the walls. Below the city walls was a shrine to Apollo; there remains a monumental block with a relief figure in a frame; the figure matches Apollo Sideton on the 4th century BCE coins of Side. On the block, Apollo carries an olive branch and another defaced object, not the usual lyre. There are mounting holes on the relief for a gilded laurel wreath and belt. The relief dates from 350-300 BCE.

The enclosed area of the shrine was outside the upper city walls; close by and well hidden in scrub are remains of a *basilica* church built with re-used blocks.

From the shrine, it's a short, steep climb up scree-covered steps to the southern city gate, a tower with a right-angled entrance below it. Inside the walls you can climb up onto the original walkway, which takes you to the southern angle of the walls. Inside the walls the ground continues to climb steeply up to the base of Bodrumkaya; in places it's scattered with pottery.

Turn NW to a wall with two towers standing to considerable height; pass through the main lower gate of the city to the *agora*; a little uphill is a three-chambered building on a slope and nearby at ground level a rather dirty open cistern. Between the terraces and the road is the base of a large temple.

Now walk up two bends of the track through scattered ruins to the upper north part of the city. Here, at the base of a stone staircase leading up onto the rock of Bodrumkaya above, is a large but overgrown area. It included an *agora* with *basilica*, a small temple and a market building whose lower storey forms a retaining wall. The large *basilica* is closest to the track; maybe the apse was demolished when the track was bulldozed. It was a huge building, over 30m long, and with three aisles divided by two rows of eight columns of the Doric order, presumably reused from an earlier building. Fragments of architrave and other dressed blocks lie around, and the position of the entrance is clear enough. It opened onto a paved *agora* with superb views over the plain. The edge of the *agora* opposite the *basilica* was formed by a *stoa* which ran over the top of a commercial building below. The north end of the building has three stories, confirmed by the beam holes for the floors, and rose above the level of the *agora*. The material is squared blocks and it was built in the Hellenistic period but repaired later.

The most interesting blocks from the *agora* are the coffered ceiling blocks, pieces of frieze and an inscription dedicating this temple to the Sebastii. The ceiling design is of masks, similar to some at Adada, and the date is 2nd century AD.

Beyond the *agora*, the track ends and you continue via a clear footpath, passing between the rock face and a magnificent stretch of wall with a tower and gate. The lower courses of masonry are cushion-shaped and are topped by square-cut blocks. The narrow gateway adjoins a tower and was closed by a gate; you can see how it fitted. The gate was repaired at a later date and there's an inscription on the upright dating the repair to the 3rd century AD. The walls themselves are much earlier.

Outside the walls is evidence of the city water supply; several rock cut cisterns of great depth.

HASGEBE - HASKIZILÖREN 7.5

Hasgebe - Haskızılören (3hrs 45mins)

This route follows the course of the Roman road which ran north from Pednelissos on the west side of the valley. Unfortunately, much of it has been destroyed and the route runs over a modern bulldozed road. After the village of Sazak, the route descends to cross a sidestream then rises to meet the modern road at a graveyard. A short walk takes you to a fish-farm at the gushing springs of Pınargözü. From here a walled, partly cobbled path climbs the hill to Haskızılören.

Follow the rough dirt track along the hillside, with a few houses of Hasgebe below/R; pass a large *çeşme* above a junction and continue on the main track to meet dirt road rising on the R. *15mins*

Continue contouring NE along the hillside, passing various side-tracks. The new dirt road has mainly obscured the old one, but leave the road for the original old path as marked. The views to the R over the river valley and to the bare peak of Bozburun beyond are pleasant. Approaching the small village of Sazak, rejoin the dirt road then turn R/down, parallel with the road and approach the village on old path, partly walled, between trees and across a terrace to pass under a wooden frame for a vine and arrive at the village road. *1hr 40mins*

Turn R and walk around a L bend, pass a mosque and rejoin the new dirt road; bear R and 400m further on turn R/E onto footpath. Follow this steeply downhill, bearing L/N to cross a stream-bed. Climb in woodland with houses on the R; continue with houses on the L then join a dirt track. Turn R/SE/uphill and follow a narrower rising track with a wooded hill on the L to meet the asphalt village road opposite a graveyard. *30mins*

Turn R and walk down the asphalt towards Pınargözü village. The turn onto a track leading to the rising old path to Haskızılören is 100m before the restaurant. *30mins*

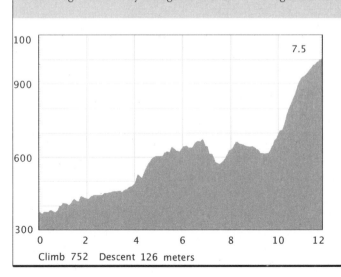

Climb 752 Descent 126 meters

Pınargözü is a straggling village on a wide, gravelly stream rushing down from the Taurus. The lower part of the village was severely damaged in flash floods one night in November 2011; six people lost their lives and the lower part of the village road and the bridge were swept away. The bridge has now been rebuilt and basic repairs completed but there is gravel and timber scattered around, showing the extent of the devastation. Below the fish farm is an old mill, still equipped with a wooden hopper and millwheel. A huge spring from the steep limestone hillside feeds multiple terraces of tanks where trout are bred; they were well above the flood. You could stop here and have a meal on the upper terrace.

From the top terrace of the fish farm, contour the hillside to the south and, above the last building, find and follow a track. 50m after, the old path to Haskızılören turns R/NW off this track - you can also reach this point from the road before the fish-farm.

5mins

Follow the footpath upwards, with trees on the R, through rocks, with the main limestone mass R. After the trees, the path runs NW then soon hairpins L to avoid scree. Past the scree, it turn NW again and becomes clearer, climbing with trees on the L and rock on the R.

30mins

Past a rock outcrop, it begins to climb terraces between fields and orchards; here the walls start and the path is very clear. It bends L and rises to the old school building on the hilltop. From the schoolyard, descend L and cross the stream; climb the far side to the asphalt road at the W edge of the village.

15mins

Ören, real name **Haskızılören**, is a large village situated on dirt road on the mountainside above Pınargözü. The muddy main street runs alongside a stream towards a mosque with seating platform. On the left is an occasionally open *kahve*; below it is the bus stop from which services depart to Pınargözü daily. There is no *bakkal*, but the villagers will supply *yufka* or other essentials. You could camp in the grounds of the disused village school, which you passed on the way up the hill.

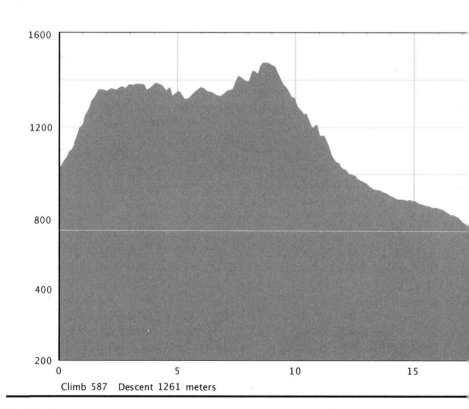

Climb 587   Descent 1261 meters

Haskızılören - Çandır (8hrs 35mins)

This walk climbs then traverses the rugged mountain range above Ören, using an old village footpath. It contours the steep NW slope on forest road, through stands of cedars, with views over Karacaören and Davraz beyond. After a pass, the route turns down the hill and follows paths along a stream to the mahalle of Yıldız. Joining the road, you pass below new mining works before turning R to follow an old road through a side-valley - this descends to the riverside where you turn R for the Çandır Nature Park. There are several camping platforms with water sources near the pass, or a smart pension and fishfarm in Çandır, or camp site at the entrance to the Park.

Take a narrow cobbled G4 footpath about 50m past the main *çeşme* on the asphalt road in Ören; it climbs steeply, running NW between fenced gardens of cottages and emerges onto farmland. Continue up on footpath, past a fenced orchard on the L, to a dirt road.   *20mins*

Turn R and follow the road around a L bend; turn L on a path between walls, climbing steeply. The path winds through bushes then follows the line of a stony stream-bed. It crosses the road, passes a small hut on the L and crosses the road again.   *30mins*

Climb L beneath pines then turn R through a gap between boulders to a grassy area and a *yalak* dated 1979. Continue L on stony hairpins, passing a couple more huts and another bend.   *20mins*

Climb steeply to the upper pastures and a junction just before a rock. Choose the R/N path, rising then contouring NW, with the huts and road below L. Crossing a pass, the path passes a *çeşme* and small pond under an overhanging tree.   *35mins*

Follow a *kanalet* around the upper side of a fenced orchard and continue N over the next ridge, then bear slightly R /NE and descend between junipers to the main forest road; turn R.   *15mins*

Follow the forest road around a steep-sided valley, passing over several stream-beds and climbing over ridge beyond then curving around a second valley. It climbs again to a major pass with extensive views over cedar and pine forest with huge mature trees and down the valleys to Karacaören lake beyond.   *1hr 20mins*

Just beyond the pass, turn L/NW onto a faint bulldozed track. Continue on footpath, descend over a rocky staircase towards a shepherd's hut then N into a tree-filled valley to pass a *çeşme* in a clearing. Bear R/NW on a path running down a stream-bed; pass between low cliffs, climb R and continue downhill to a clear, grassy old road. You are now in a broad, forested terraced valley, edged with cliffs, sloping all the way down to Yıldız, visible below. Follow the old road R/NE with terraces on the L; at the bottom of the terraces pass between trees and follow track to a stream bed: descend a gravelly patch to cross a dirt road.   *1hr 20mins*

Continue NW/downhill, following the stream bed through

7.6

20

trees then scrub to meet the track again on a bend. Follow the track for 1km; the stream is below L and the trees on the slope beyond have been recently felled. Where the valley narrows, descend to lower track and cross the stream towards a fenced enclosure.

35mins

Turn R and follow faint Grade 2 track between the fence and the stream. In places the path re-crosses to the R bank to avoid rock walls, but soon reverts to the L bank again. After a km, on a flat open area, the path turns R/N and crosses the stream.

40mins

It rises over low banks of shaley soil, gradually becoming clearer, then meets a village road just before Yıldız. Walk through the village and continue for a km to meet the main dirt road.

1hr 5mins

The next section is nearly 3km on dirt road below several marble mines; the heavy lorries and noisy machinery make the route unpleasant, but there is no alternative path.

45mins

Just after a *çeşme* under a mulberry tree, take a G2 path descending steeply L/NW to a grassy area scattered with stone blocks of ancient buildings. Just beyond is a hillock with the remains of a church. Descend an old path through woodland to a *yalak* and turn L on the road. 100m further on, turn R and cross a stream bed to a G2 track which contours, then rises to an electricity pylon, then descends the pylon line to the road again.

25mins

Turn R and follow dirt road to a bend; turn E and take a track upwards; as it approaches an open area turn sharp L /NNW onto a footpath which climbs to open fields. Cross a hilltop and descend R, below a rock to a path along woodland. Follow this around a bend to cut a track.

15mins

On the far side is a valley descending between rock walls to join the Çandır valley. A Roman road once ran down the valley; our route follows footpath NNW then merges with wide clear old road, which descends to the stream. Cross it then cross again below trees, continuing over a sidestream with the main stream below/L. The path soon becomes clear again and runs almost straight to meet a dirt road in the valley.

40mins

If you walk down to the bridge and turn L, you soon reach Çandır village; alternatively there are pensions ahead and to the R.

Çandır, now a forestry town, was once the centre of the rich agricultural area drowned by flooding the lake. An original Selçuk bridge also disappeared into the waters. Çandir's economy is now based on fish farming, forestry and tourism. The forestry department have offices and a visitors' house on the canyon road; nearby is a *kahve* and a couple of markets. A daily bus to Eğirdir leaves at 6am from the central crossroads.

Çandır - Çuruk via the Yazılı canyon rim (5hrs 25mins)

The Roman road from Çandır originally ran close to the river through the canyon; until recently (probably until an earthquake of 1953) a horse and cart could pass from Sütçüler to Çandır. In late summer it is still possible to walk through the canyon. An asphalt road links Çandır to the Nature Park, but the route follows a dirt track on the east bank of the river; in the Park this links with the Roman road. Our marked, narrow footpath climbs through forest up the canyon side, circles the rim and descends to the tiny village of Çuruk. The section over the canyon rim crosses two rock walls with the aid of hand-holds; they could be slippery in bad weather. From the rim you can see down into the canyon, over the other gorges, and across the lake to the mountains beyond. Take enough water as there is none en-route.

Turn R on the dirt road and follow it with the river below/R. Before the road swings R, turn L and follow a track parallel with the river then R and across a bridge to rejoin the road. Turn L and walk for a km to an open area with a small building on the L. Here is a path over a wooden bridge to a fish-farm, restaurant and pension on the W bank. *40mins*

Continuing NW on the E bank, follow a path which marks the route of a water-pipe around a bend; it becomes rougher then is blocked by a pile of rocks. *45mins*

The easiest way around to get around the rocks is to descend to the stream and balance along the large bore pipe below them. On the far side, follow the track to a wooden bridge crossing the river to the restaurant at the entrance to the Park; alternatively you could continue for 80m to a ford leading to the carpark on the west bank. *20mins*

From the carpark, a path squeezes along rock walls above the river, which at this point runs between eroded rocks 20m below. It crosses a bridge over a side stream, then a second one over the main canyon; here it meets the Roman road on the E side of the river. Continue N on a stretch of the original Roman road through the canyon, marked by Greek inscriptions cut in the walls and niches for offerings. The canyon widens out to form a green haven surrounded by high rock walls and forest; just before here, the route climbs R/E up a side-track. *30mins*

This track levels off, turns N and comes to a gully. Turn R on a faint path which zigzags up the wide shallow valley with a dry stream bed on the R. It leaves the stream to cross a low outcrop of rock then resumes zigzagging up to a low stone wall. Here, turn slightly L to a small shepherd hut and the ruins of a fortification on the pass, Asar Boyun. *45mins*

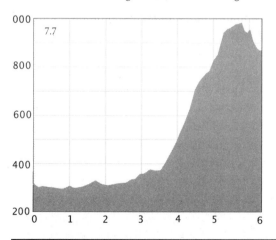

Climb 675   Descent 127 meters

Yazılı Canyon Nature Park occupies about 600 hectares of mixed forest and scrub north of Çandır alongside the river and into the canyon. The canyon banks are very steep and high and clad with pine species right up to the cliffs of the canyon rim. The canyon varies in depth from 100 to 400m. Above the rim are areas of deeply eroded limestone rocks clad with maquis. At the entrance is an open-air restaurant with car-park, toilets and showers; there are a few tents to rent here, or you could pitch your own tent. There is a large open meadow inside the canyon, it's a good picnic and camping place except on summer weekends when it's crowded with barbecuing locals. Along the river itself are several massive *çınar* of great age; there are sandbanks and pools below where it's possible to swim. The river is an excellent place for birdwatching; in the course of an afternoon we spotted pied wagtails, a dipper, kingfishers, coal and great tits, collared flycatcher, blackcaps and three other warblers, a white-backed woodpecker and green sandpiper. Because the sides are so steep, visitors mainly stay in the canyon bottom, which means that the cliffs are a haven for wildlife. A flock of wild goats, griffon vultures, wallcreeper and rock nuthatch can be seen from the upper path.

The park was protected largely because the rock walls carry various inscriptions which mark the course of the Roman road (known locally as the King's road). The road once ran through the canyon itself, crossing the river in several places. There used to be two exits, one to Çürük and the other over a zigzag paved road to Kutu, north of the canyon. After the loss of this route, both Sütçüler and Çandır declined in importance.

15mins	The path climbs steeply L/NE towards the sheer rock face above. Bear L with the rock face above/R and continue across sloping slabs to an outcrop with expansive views.
35mins	Descend from the viewpoint and continue between scrub, across scree and two low side-ridges. Pass a scree slope with a large rock in the centre to a more prominent and steep ridge, with no obvious crossing place. Follow the narrow marked path along a ledge, just above a large pine, over the ridge and descend rock steps to the path below – about 2 minutes careful scrambling.
40mins	The path climbs steeply then follows the canyon wall for about 100m towards a shallow cave and another side ridge. Climb up the marked steps into the cave and L over the ridge on a ledge. A path zigzags up toward the rock wall above and climbs a short gully on steps to the ridgetop.
15mins	From the top are views are over the forested canyon slopes and the junction of the two northern canyons (Değirmen Dere and Bağırsak Dere; E and W respectively) with the Çandır Canyon. Beyond is a wide panorama over the lake of Karacaören and the mountains beyond; Davraz is on the horizon on the R. The path winds around rocks, heading L/NE towards a low ridge with a small solitary tree.
40mins	The path continues diagonally down R/NE along rock ledges but widens, circles R/SE, and descends straight between trees. The final descent to the farmland at Çuruk is down rock steps and a narrow path contouring to a worn forest road. Continue down a bend of the road towards a fenced orchard below.

You can now continue to Adada either via Sutçuler (7.8A, 7.9A) or Müezzinler (7.8B, 7.9B). Sutçuler has accommodation, internet access and a bank. Müezzinler has none of these, but the route is closer to the original Roman road.

Çuruk has six houses, only used in summer, near to the top of the valley. If you turn R and walk up the forest road you pass a *yalak* then the first house. A Roman road ran from Pınargözü to the head of the Çuruk valley and continued down the valley and across the canyon towards Müezzinler and Adada.

Çuruk - Sütçüler (3hrs 15mins)

From Çürük, *kaldırım,* tracks and asphalt lead down to Sütçüler hydroelectric station and an old mill; from there a mill track climbs through byways lined with fine traditional houses to the Selçuk mosque in the centre of Sütçüler.

Follow the forest road E above an orchard, across a stream, then L/up on a clearer road with a drop to the canyon on the L. Continue to a concreted *çeşme,* just L/below the road. 200m after this, on a bend, turn L/N onto a steep goat track. *40mins*

Descend the path, becoming paved *kaldırım,* to the village of Yeşildere; bear L and continue down the main village street to the mosque. *20mins*

Yeşildere is a *mahalle* of Sütçüler, not a village in its own right. It has a few old houses in well-stocked gardens, a simple, modern mosque with a water supply, a stone bread oven and a milling stone in the man street. The inhabitants use the old road to reach their other homes at Çuruk.

Leave the mosque on the R and continue E through the fence on a stony path to the bed of a stream below. Cross the stream under a *çınar* and climb towards a tree-filled graveyard. Circle the graveyard with the fence on the R until you come to a *çeşme* on the upper side. *25mins*

Climb uphill to the access track and walk up towards the road, turning first L then R. *40mins*

Walk down the asphalt into the Değirmen valley, passing the electricity generating station to a road bridge over the river. *20mins*

The **old mill** is below the level of the road; above are sluices and an incoming mill stream; millwheels and wooden paddlewheels can be seen through gaps in the corrugated iron roof. If you walk E/upstream for 30 minutes, you come to a secluded pool amidst trees, with a waterfall and gravel beach - ideal for swimming.

Continue E on a shady, level path following the shallow stream beneath trees, between garden walls towards another bridge. Cross the stream to an open area used as a car park then continue NNW/up a rough track and cross an irrigation ditch towards a walled garden. Turn R along the wall to a junction of dirt roads by an electricity distribution station. *15mins*

Continue N then turn L/NW/down onto the original mill path, which runs above and parallel with the stream below to an area where the bank has collapsed; turn L/N and cross the stream below. Climb diagonally to a path below a stone-wall; turn R onto this to meet a track running down to the water. Re-cross the stream, turn uphill on the E bank and 100m later re-cross onto tractor track. *15mins*

Only 50m on, turn R onto an old walled road; in places it's overgrown and the walls have collapsed, but it's unmistakably part of the mill track. After 400m, at its end, climb diagonally L towards a wire fence surrounding a waste water treatment works. Walk up a wide track following a line of concrete pipes and drain covers, bearing L around the wire, then R to a junction by a house. Turn L/N onto a rising unsurfaced road with old houses then R and round a L bend and R at a *çeşme.* At the next R turn, by a large modern house, turn L/NNW onto a walled path. *15mins*

Walk above a row of gardens and cross a wooden footbridge over a stream. Climb R up a slope to a road and turn R towards the main mosque, which rises high above the houses. Climb L/up a concrete ramp, and turn L again towards the mosque. Turn R to emerge on the main square between the bank and the mosque, opposite to the tea gardens.

15mins

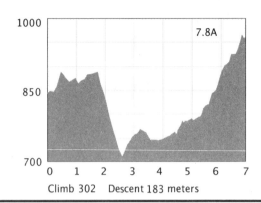

Climb 302   Descent 183 meters

Sütçüler dates at least from Roman times. On the hill near the new hospital is Taşkapı, a walled enclosure with a gate, which seems from the dressed stone to be Roman in origin; other remains are scattered around. On a hill in Asar Mahalle is an early Byzantine castle with outer walls and towers still standing. Sütçüler was hit by an earthquake in 1930 and many people moved to İstanbul or elsewhere but some attractive half-timbered houses are still scattered in orchards. Only 10 years ago, Sütçüler had several hotels - today, the only pension in town is 300m NW, on the Eğirdir road, opposite the Jandarma building. Life now centres around the central square; with *kahve* and the square Selçuk mosque, much restored and now very plain inside and out. Ziraat Bank, next to the Selçuk mosque, offers money-changing services and nearby is an internet cafe. There are fruit stalls every day on the square, but on Fridays there is a market with local produce, hardware and textiles.

Shops are small but adequate; several markets, two greengrocers, a pastry shop up the hill, a shoe-shop, a small *lokanta*, but no camping gaz. A petrol station will fill up your stove.

Buses to Isparta via Eğirdir run several times per day; the first one leaves at 7am. Less-frequent buses run to Antalya, some via Çandır.

Sütçüler - Adada (4hrs 50mins)

This route is manly on dirt road with some pleasant paths. It runs first along the main road then climbs and contours a west-facing hillside overlooking the canyon before descending to cross a second village road. You climb two low lines of hills before the plain below Adada. Here it joins a paved Roman road rising up the valley side in a long curve to the ruins of Adada. This is the most spectacular old road on the whole of the St Paul Trail.

From the centre of Sütçüler, either get a lift, a taxi or walk 2.5km N/uphill out of town on the Eğirdir road. If you walk, you can use the lower road past the graveyards to the second, new mosque.

1hr 10mins

Turn R/NNE onto rising, unsurfaced road and follow it for 1km to a junction with a *yalak*. (7.7B joins here) Turn R/ENE and continue for 1.5km over a low hill and down to a junction and R bend.

50mins

Turn L/NW, ignoring the wider track into the valley bottom, onto a narrower, tree-lined old road which swings R, descends the valley and crosses a gravelly stream bed. On the far side it continues with a graveyard on the R to an asphalt road; turn L/W.

40mins

Walk 800m along the valley bottom to a sharp L bend. Turn R/N and climb towards a small village; take the 2nd L/NNW turn onto a dirt road becoming path.

1hr 10mins

Climb along the slope of the hill, passing a few stone houses and after the last house bear L onto an old, walled road above the village. At the end, cross the pass at the lowest point; continue down to find a path running on the L slope into the valley beyond. It joins a much wider track.

50mins

Almost immediately, where this swings L, continue down/NW, cross a stream to a track on the far side. Turn R with fields on the R; at the end turn L onto a goat path rising amongst scrub to a second hilltop. Descend with woodland on the L to a plain beyond and continue on faint paths to a ford over a stream-bed just below the asphalt road.

40mins

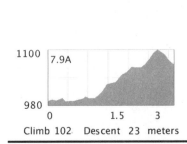

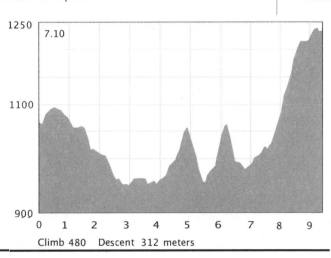

Turn R onto a walled old road studded with large pines and follow this to cross a second stream bed. A few metres on, turn R/NE onto a faint path rising over terraces to meet the Roman road. The 2m wide road, made of enormous slabs, rises on the L/W bank of a stony valley; follow it uphill/NE then NW towards the site of Adada. Approaching the site, climb L, away from the streambed towards the ruins of a church and earlier remains. Continue past various Roman walls to reach the site above the *agora*.

50mins

Sağrak is a village on the west slope of the valley opposite Adada. It's spread out above the main road and the old school building has been converted to provide accommodation for trekkers. The two watchmen at the site, Mustafa and Ramazan, have organised a group of village women to run it. Meals are served in a classroom using the original wooden tables and chairs.

Çuruk – Müezzinler (5hrs 5mins)

This route is mainly on Roman road; parts are steep and difficult, but the views are great. It descends a steep path into the canyon, crosses the stream then climbs the far side first on path then on zigzag Roman road. It meanders to a farm then turns upwards into a valley between hills to cross the village road. It climbs the Değirmendere valley to Müezzinler, via old road, steep path and old road again.

From the orchard, walk downhill on difficult, zigzag path between rock masses and through woodland towards the canyon. Keep close to the L rock wall then bear R/N to the stream in the valley bottom; cross carefully. Climb the far bank through pines, keeping to the R of the side valley and find traces of the rising Roman road, zigzagging N up the hill. There is a difficult section where the road is damaged and you have to climb over a rock fall but from then the road is made of slabs and climbs NE in built-up zigzags. It emerges from undergrowth and bears R/S over a stream-bed.

2hr 30mins

The Roman road is now lost in undergrowth, so the route follows terraces, climbs a rocky outcrop and passes a well with steps into the depths. It rejoins the Roman road climbing NE with a stream on the R and follows this towards the farmhouse at Kutu.

35mins

Kutu has a couple of neat farmhouses and an old house. A Roman road run parallel with the dirt road that rises through woodland towards Müezzinler but tree-cutting has made it difficult to find or follow.

Just before the farmhouse turn NW over fields towards a gap between two wooded hills. Join a straight footpath running on the banks of a small stream through woodland. Approaching the top of the hill, the path runs through scrub and descends to an asphalt road. Cross straight over the road and cut off a bend, rejoining the road.

35mins

Turn R/NNE onto a wide old road contouring the valley side above the Değirmendere canyon. At a sharp L bend, turn R/ENE and climb up a stream bed, turning L/N and continuing steeply upwards through trees to meet an old road rising from the bottom of the canyon.

30mins

Turn R/NE and continue to pass over the canyon rim at a small stone hut, then turn E through forest, crossing a narrow sloping field. Bear L/NE and follow the Müezzinler graveyard wall to the road; turn R/E and walk to the *çeşme* and school.

55mins

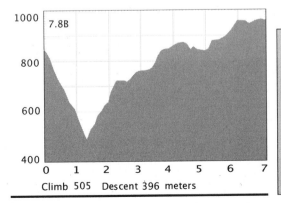

Climb 505 Descent 396 meters

Müezzinler is a quiet farming village, consisting mainly of old stone houses, around a crossroads with school, *çeşme* and graveyard. It's on the plateau close to the junction of the two canyons and the land falls away nearly all around. A Roman road traversed the village to the old city between here and Sütçüler, only 4km away. There is no *bakkal* or accommodation, not even a regular bus.

Müezzinler - Adada (6hrs 10mins)

This route, mainly on old road, passes through woodland, crosses the main road and climbs to a track contouring the hillside then descending to cross a second village road. You cross two low lines of hills to the plain below Adada. Here you join a paved Roman road rising up the valley side in a long curve to the ruins of Adada. This is the most spectacular old road on the whole of the St Paul Trail.

30mins

From the *çeşme* at Müezzinler, turn N along the tarmac road to Sütçüler. Where the road swings R, carry straight on down a track which skirts the edge of woodland, and continues between hedges to turn L/N on a dirt road in a dry valley bottom.

35mins

100m further on, turn R/N onto a rising path running parallel to the dirt road and bearing R onto wider old track. Rejoin the dirt road, immediately branch L and, in a dip, turn L/N onto a narrow path.

15mins

Continue through old woodland, passing overgrown walls in the undergowth, then descend and cross a stream bed. At a tractor track turn R/SE and continue to a field then past a solitary pine to the asphalt road.

Turn R, cross the road and find a path rising through woodland to a lone house. Turn L/E on a wide path climbing gently up a ridge. Pass through a gap between trees, cross farmland, climbing towards the first house and join a dirt road. At a junction by a spring turn L/NE to another house; walk around this house to a clear, walled path. Cross one shallow stream bed and continue to a second; turn L, over the stream and up the far bank. Here the path is almost lost; pass below a farmhouse on the R and cross open fields to meet the dirt road immediately

1hr 30mins

before a junction and *yalak*.

3hr 20mins

Turn L and follow section 7.9a to Adada.

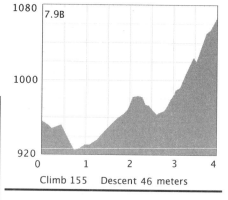

Climb 155   Descent 46 meters

8   BEŞKONAK - ADADA

Beşkonak and rafting on the Köprülü River

The centre of Beşkonak is about 4km below the bridge, on the E bank. On the road are a couple of shops with the usual groceries, cigarettes, chocolate etc; there are more about a km ahead. Minibuses run to and from Serik bus station several times per day, a journey time of 1hr 30mins. North of Beşkonak, past the graveyard, along the riverside is a mixture of boat storage sheds and trout restaurants; the former are for the rafts and canoes which ply the rapids downstream of the canyon, the latter for their customers. The main rafting season is May to October, but some companies offer wetsuits and thus extend the season; very early season rafting is only for the experienced. Boats are either inflatables seating 10 and captained by a guide, or two-person inflatable canoes.

In season, rafters come from the holiday villages and hotels along the coast and are swept down the shallow, easy river. In April / May, when the snowmelt is pouring into the higher reaches of the river, rafting is a real adventure; by August it resembles a splash in a crowded toddlers' paddling pool.

The 'course' runs downstream from below the bridge to a major rapid just above the bridge to Karabük, and takes about 3hrs. Customers can swim, jump off the first bridge, play water games and have lunch, either a barbecue or a riverside restaurant meal.

If you want to spend a day rafting before you start your walk, a number of firms can offer you a day on the river at reasonable prices, including lunch; the extras, such as drinks, are very expensive. They can return you to the start after your day out.

Adam kayalar / men rocks, eroded pinnacles of rock topped by harder boulders, surround the Köprülü river and Selge. The capstones are made from a layer of conglomerate bonded by silica, more water resistant than the layers beneath. Similar to the famous Cappadocian fairy chimneys, they are spread over a wide area and must have been a formidable defense for the city of Selge. The rocks provide a haven for small animals, such as rock martins, Persian squirrels, hedgehogs and porcupines and between them grow strawberry trees, *arbutus andranche* and *arbutus unedo*, with beautiful reddish bark shedding to show a pistachio-green underlayer.

Oluk Köprüsü - Selge (5hrs 15mins)

This route first follows the river, starting high then descending to the water's edge. It passes a farmhouse / pension amid farmland and crosses to the W bank via a natural bridge. A steep, bouldery track climbs the canyon wall then continues between strange rock outcrops on a mixture of tracks to Selge, a Roman site set high above magnificent forest and the canyon itself. With a full backpack the climb is hard; you could take a daypack and ask a bus driver to take your main pack to Selge.

From the Oluk bridge road, turn R/N up onto a rising path, which cuts the corner of the main S-N road through the canyon. Cross the road and cut the next two bends to arrive at a large flat area with views over the canyon. Beyond this viewpoint, take a path descending L into a side valley and a steel bridge.

20 mins

Turn L on unsurfaced road; after the bridge turn L onto woodland path which rises steeply and cuts the first bend. Rejoin the road and walk up the next bends; where the road levels off, turn L/W onto a fire road.

20 mins

Walk down the track for 100m to the rim of the canyon; there are views down the sheer sides and to the forested far bank. Turn R/N, parallel with the canyon. If you look over the rim, below here is a natural bridge, where a boulder has fallen from the canyon walls and wedged itself above the water; there are traces of steps running down the canyon sides and over the rock. Where the track ends, turn L down a sandy gully running towards the river's edge; turn R and pass just above a *çınar* on the water's edge.

15 mins

Find a clear track which runs R/N above the waterline, crosses a side stream and climbs gently through woodland towards Tevfik's house. Keep L at a junction, continue through a gate, past a small stone building and cross a large open yard to the main house.

20 mins

> **Tevfik's pension** is a former farmhouse belonging to the owner of a rafting company; they have accommodation in wooden cabins and the main house and an open-air restaurant. Just beyond the house is a level field, once a courtyard, with the remains of the curved walls of the apse of an early church at one end and other buildings opposite - maybe the remains of an early monastery?

Continue N, going downhill between Tevfik's house and the restaurant, on a path which crosses a stream bed to the open field; turn L/NNW on tractor track. Cross a side stream and pass a shepherd's hut on the L.

25 mins

The track, now fenced, crosses a second stream and turns L to arrive at Yer Köprüsü, the natural bridge over the Köprülü Cay.

25 mins

> Above **Yer Köprüsü** the river valley is wide and the water is shallow; it's a favourite fishing spot. The water drops about 5m below the wide natural bridge; it emerges downstream swirling and bubbling into a pool. It's a great picnic and swimming place.

Cross the bridge and continue up the tractor track for 150 mtres. Where a side gully meets the track, follow a footpath R/up towards the cliffs of the valley.

10 mins

At the wall, cross the top of a gully on the L and follow the path SW to a junction. Keep R/SW up on a steep L diagonal, climbing over steps and ledges and, near the top, through a barrier. The views become more spectacular as you climb; the river lies in bright blue bends below you, across a patchwork of cultivated fields. Tevfik's house is clearly visible, but there is little sign of other habitation.

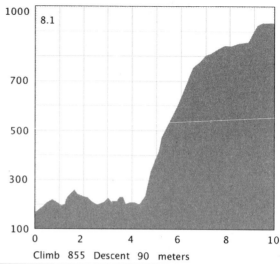

50 mins

After a flat area, climb W into a narrow valley with woodland L, then pass through a gap between rocks to an area of Adam kayalar. The path swings NNW and climbs up terraces to more pinnacled rocks and into trees. Now clearer, the path bears L/NW and rises through fields and terraces to meet a dirt road in a valley.

1hr 20mins

Turn L/WSW, passing a *çeşme* and the houses of Akarca Mahallesi. Turn L and cut off a bend; continue with the road on the R to another group of houses and a *çeşme*; rejoin the road.

25mins

The theatre is straight ahead; continue on footpath across a level area to the *bakkal* and then turn R on the dirt road to the theatre.

15mins

The theatre towers above **Selge**; although the stage building is in ruins, the seating backs onto the hillside and has 30 rows below and 15 above the *diazoma*. The stage building, of 2nd century AD, was a classic Roman design with five doors and a colonnaded facade. From the top row of seats is a spectacular view east across the Köprülü valley.

Adjoining the theatre, and with a few village houses built inside it, is the stadium. One of the long sides forms the wall edging the village road. Only a couple of rows are visible each side; the seating was reused to build the village houses.

At the SW end of the stadium are baths, quite overgrown and filled with rubble. A path leads to the ruined city on top of the crescent hill, surrounded by a defensive wall of ashlar masonry with towers along it.

On the W summit are two temples; presumably the huge (17x 34m) peripteral temple was the Zeus temple known as the Kesbedion. It had 6 columns on the short and 11 on the long side, and is of the 3rd century BCE. It's very similar to the temple which stood in the *temenos* at Men Askaenos at Antioch in Pisidia. The other temple was probably, on the basis of a nearby inscription, dedicated to Artemis.

Behind here is a huge round cistern where the aqueduct terminated. A porticoed street led along the ridge to a paved *agora* with *stoas* on three sides and a market building is similar to, but not so well preserved, as the one at Pednelissos. A *triskeles* symbol reminiscent of those at Adada and Aspendos, can be seen on a stone block.

Below on the hillside is a *nymphaeum* with a cistern behind it, and nearby are graves of various types, including some hollowed-out boulders once capped by flat stones.

The west aqueduct crossed the Değirmen Dere 1km W of the ruins and another bridge at Okuzbuku to a spring called Kuma Suyu Pınarı. Another northern aqueduct with a bridge crossed the slopes of Yoncalıuşak Tepe. Aspendos' and Selge's aqueducts were probably wrecked in the same earthquake.

The village of **Altınkaya** or Selge occupies a shallow bowl west of the old city. The many fragments of old Selge add to the charm of the stone village houses. Income is mainly from goat farming and sale of handicrafts. There is a large primary school but older children board at Beşkonak or Serik, so in termtime there is a notable absence of teenagers. The village has small *bakkals*, seasonal cafes and accommodation in a village house. A daily bus to Serik leaves from Oluk Mahallesi at 7am and returns at 2pm; it takes 2 hours.

Selge - history

Selge is perched above the Köprülü Canyon on a crescent hill with the theatre at the NE end. Beyond the surrounding farmland, the ground drops away on the east, south and north, giving a well-defended position with difficult access. A road from Pednelissos in the west continued to the bridges over the Köprülü Cay. From the Oluk bridge, a road ran down the river to Aspendos, following the aqueduct into the city. Another ran N to Çaltepe, where the footings of an old bridge are visible. Selge is naturally short of water but an aqueduct brought water from Bozburun; the extensive terraces must have conserved water and enabled cultivation of a wheat crop.

In 1842 von Schonborn, and in 1875 Hurschfeld visited and described Selge; in 1890, Lanckoronski drew a map, but it has never been excavated.

According to Strabo, Selge's founder was Calchas, associate of Mopsus, the legendary founder of Aspendos. The forests must have attracted early settlers; trees could easily be floated down to Aspendos and were much in demand for shipbuilding, especially in Egypt. Strabo mentions the harvesting of useful plants, in particular an iris, which provided a liquid used in massage, and storax which exuded a gum used as a substitute for incense. Other important products were olive oil and wine; the land around Selge was probably used for the summer pasturing of Aspendos' famous horses.

Selge minted coins very early; they were almost exact replicas of Aspendos' silver *staters*, with the wrestlers and slinger motifs. The name is given as Stlegiys, an ancient Pisidian word which was used until the Persian conquest.

According to Arrian, Selge signed an alliance with Alexander. Polybius recounts this interesting little tale: In 218 BCE, Selge, with 20,000 soldiers (undoubtedy an exaggerated number), besieged Pednelissos. Pednelissos appealed to Achaeus, uncle of Antiochos III, for help; he sent his general Garsyeris, with 6,500 men but Selge blocked the passes and Garsyeris retreated. The Selgean troops, assuming victory, went home to start the harvest.

Garsyeris immediately returned, garrisoned the pass of Kretopolis (presumably between Selge and Pednelissos) and gathered more troops. Meanwhile, Selge resumed the seige and tried unsuccessfully to recapture the pass. Garsyeris tried to smuggle troops laden with bags of wheat into Pednelissos. Selge's troops intercepted them but the Pednelissans burst out of the city and, with Garsyeris, captured or killed half Selge's men; the rest fled.

It was now Garsyeris' turn to beseige Selge. Achaeus arrived to negotiate, planning to seize the main temple (the Kesbedion) while talks were in progress. He was driven back, but the two sides eventually negotiated a treaty under which Selge had to pay a total of 700 talents and free their prisoners.

The whole story must be exaggerated - present day Selge couldn't produce 200 fit men, let alone 20,000, and 700 talents is far more than the fine Alexander imposed on his conquests.

With the rest of Pamphylia, in 133BCE, Selge came under control of the wealthy Attalids. Later, although nominally part of the Roman Empire, it minted its own coins until the 3rd century. In the late 4th century, an earthquake damaged the aqueducts and they were never repaired. In 399 AD, Goth settlers attacked; Selge fought them off.

In the 5th and 6th century, people from Aspendos may have taken refuge from the plague and pirates inside Selge's walls. But after the 6th century only a village remained.

8.2 | SELGE - ÇALTEPE

Selge - Çaltepe (7hrs 45mins)

This route starts as a cross-country trek on a mixture of footpaths, dirt roads and old Roman road, often in beautiful mature forest. It bypasses the district of Ören then passes through Delisarnıç and Kestanelik, two small villages. After switchbacking over several ridges, the route descends the Sarp Yolu, an ancient paved trail used by the shepherds who move between Çaltepe and higher pastures.

20mins

Leave Selge on a footpath L of the theatre, past a pumphouse and down past two graves cut from boulders to the village road. Turn L and walk around a R bend over the head of a valley. Just after a house on the R, turn R/down and join a footpath below and parallel with the road.

35mins

Follow this horizontally then, after the trees on the far bank, turn down, cross a stream bed and, on the far side, climb an old road, well built of large slabs and walled for much of its length. At the top of the hill, turn R onto an unsurfaced road linking Ören with Delisarnıç.

5mins

Pass the village graveyard and, just before a L bend, turn R/down through a gate.

20mins

Follow a narrow path down, cross a horizontal track and continue down to cross the stream-bed. Climb the opposite valley across terraces with trees on the R and cross a clearer path coming from some cottages. The path runs N in a valley with rounded conglomerate cliffs and boulders on each side to a clear cross-ways.

15mins

Turn R/NNE onto a track which soon joins a well-made old road passing between boulders and across an open area. Continue slightly upwards to a rocky pass, bear R and at a junction turn L along the foot of a rocky cliff to another pass.

25mins

Pass through the rocks, turn L and descends well-made steps into a E-sloping valley. Continue NE and pass through a gap between rocks.

20mins

The next valley is deeper, and has excellent views down R through the oak trees towards the canyon. The path zigzags steeply down the valley side, bears L to a stony stream bed and continues up the far side of the stream to a pass.

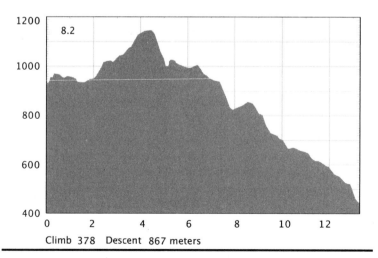

Climb 378   Descent 867 meters

It descends NNE between rock outcrops then turns L/NNW, descending gently and winding through rocks, trees and grapevines. At a rocky stream-bed, turn R for 50m and continue NNE on the far side, climbing to a large field. Bear R around large oak trees to a fenced tractor track; turn L and walk past the fenced graveyard of Delisarnıç to the unsurfaced village road.

1hr 20mins

Delisarnıç (a contraction of *deliksarnıç*/well in a hole, an exact description of the natural water sources), has several neat new houses with gardens and older ones set between the boulders. On the R is a new mosque, and opposite a water supply fed by a natural well between boulders. In late summer, when the water dries up, the villagers move down the valley.

Turn R and walk to the far end of the village. At the last house the road rises and bends sharp L. Turn R/down and cross a small field into a narrow valley which descends to a streambed. Turn R/NE and follow the stream down to a junction.

25mins

Leave the stream going NNW over a low rise then continue downhill, following a smaller stream to an open area. Look for telegraph posts; near them turn L/N and cross a wide gravel streambed to join an asphalt road; turn L/NNW and walk to the village of Kestanelik.

30mins

Kestanelik is named after the sweet chestnut trees which dwarf the old houses. It's on the road between the larger village of Ballıbuçak, on the slopes of Bozburun Dağı, and a bridge over the canyon leading to the main road on the far side. A café, occasionally open, is on the R of the point where you join the road.

Before the road crosses the stream-bed, turn R/E onto a field path running towards a huge, many-branched chestnut tree. The path passes through a gate and past a cottage the climbs small stone-walled terraces over a low pass; this area is known as Eynes Mevkii.

15mins

At a junction, take the fainter R/SE path down towards the road; turn L/NE and continue down through forest, to the head of terraced fields on the L, passing a well, then a deserted cottage.

20mins

Continue R past a second well in a crack between rocks passing a second terraced area to a level field with a double line of collapsed wooden fence on the R. On the far side, climb the bank and keep R/NNE on good path.

30mins

Descend a wooded stream bed to a junction of two streams at a small level area between rocks. Turn L, cross the side valley and continue up a clear stone-stepped *kaldırım*. This is the start of the Sarp Yolu / steep road, which runs high on the L valley slope down to Çaltepe. The track itself is partly paved, and switchbacks over the sharp side ridges.

10mins

At the top of the steps, the path swings R/NE and the paving disappears; continue on goat trails between junipers across a limestone slabbed slope, passing below shepherd cottages then above a large sheep pen.

45mins

Turn R/down a zigzag path to two boarded wells on a grassy area, then go NE down a faint path between rocks to a forested stream bed. Almost immediately follow a partly-paved path zigzagging L/up to a well-used *kaldırım*, undulating ENE between junipers until you see the village of Çaltepe in level fields below the scrubby hillside.

20mins

The path descends a ramp of perfectly placed stones then meets the new dirt road. Cross the road and descend R; rejoin the road and continue diagonally down to reach the village square and the *bakkal.*

40mins

Çaltepe is a small town on the valley floor at the foot of the limestone slopes. An unsurfaced road leads W to a bridge over the Köprülü Çay and continues to reach the main N-S asphalt road about 2km from the town. Off this road, to the S, there are ruins of baths and a small fort on a bluff over the canyon.

On the upper slopes of Hopbilla Tepe and Eşekkiri Tepe, the two hills to the NW, the villagers collect wild *kekik /* oregano, bag it up, bring it down by mule, dry it and and ship it to Italian and other consumers. The village population of mules almost exceeds the human population; each family's income depends on the number of mule-loads of oregano it can get down from the mountain during the limited season.

The oregano co-operative has a building on the square, opposite the *bakkal.* The pleasant pension is about 1km SSE across the river - the quickest route is to take the track SE to the river and wade across.

Except on Sundays, a *dolmuş* runs down the canyon via Ballıbuçak and Delisarnıç to Serik early in the morning and returns in the afternoon.

At Çaltepe, the route divides - you can either cross Hopbilla Tepe to Kozdere, Çimenova, Beydili and Çukurca, a beautiful, strenuous, isolated route partly through cedar forest (8.3b-8.4b). The alternative runs along the river to Değirmenözü village then climbs a hill to ruins and descends again to Çukurca (8.3a-8.4a). The second route is shorter, easier, allows you to swim but is not so spectacular.

Çaltepe - Değirmenözü (6 hrs 30mins)

This route runs along the riverbank northeast to Değirmenözü. Most is level and easy walking, but in a few places the route has to leave the river to climb over limestone hills; the first section is fairly rough and another has a steep descent down rough rock steps. The bridge at Değirmenözü no longer exists so you have to cross the river by wading - the crossing is wide and easy.

From the square at Çaltepe take the tractor track going NE past a few houses and a water-point to an open riverside field. Cross this on fainter tractor track, passing through trees then a large oak on the L to the point where the track rises into scrub. *15mins*

Follow footpath above the river, descend to a broken concrete *kanalet* to level fields. Continue on track above the river until the limestone slopes come right down to the bank; continue on wide gravel bank between the rock and the water. Find the continuation of the track below large *çinars* at the waterside, cross a gravelly side-gulley and continue on a path above the river towards a rock outcrop. *1hr 40mins*

The next section follows a path across rocks to a gravel beach then continues beneath *çinars* past sheep-pens, just above the river to another level area. Continue along the river, which is lined with trees, and follow a gap below another limestone ridge to another level plain. *30mins*

Again, follow the river-bank to a rougher area and continue on narrow path through trees close to the water. The path then turns L/N up over rough steps on broken limestone with scrub growing in the crevices. It continues above the river then descends to the riverside. It almost immediately again climbs, this time 50m above the river, then descends to a valley, crosses a low ridge and descends L/W through pine trees to the river again. *1hr*

The path undulates along the river over sandy path, turning R/N and climbing to the top of a sandy hill. It descends to cross a streambed then continues along the riverbank to a place where the river emerges from a gorge. Here, climb N diagonally to a gap in the ridge above the gorge. Passing through the gap, turn L/W on a ledge then descend a steep staircase to oak woods in the bottom of a side-valley. *45mins*

Cross the valley going N and climb to join a paved path on the far side. Turn R/ESE and climb the hill diagonally to a gap between rocks. Descending slightly, as the road emerges from the rocks, you can turn R and follow the Roman road, paved in huge slabs, towards the place where the original bridge crossed the river. In the rock face on the far side is a grave with carvings around it, including a man between two goats. Return to the path. *25mins*

Continue down wide, stony path to the riverside and continue under a *çinar*. Değirmenözü is on the far side - cross the river here and walk to the village road. Turn L for the village centre. *20mins*

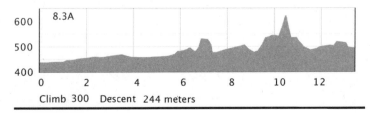

600
500
400

8.3A

0   2   4   6   8   10   12

Climb 300   Descent 244 meters

Değirmenözü is a village of about 200 people partly on level ground along the river, partly on the slope to the N. It is at the junction with a side-stream, which issues from a cave just E of the village; it is this stream which powered the mills which gave the village its name. On a night in November 2011, the village was woken by a powerful flood, caused by storms higher up the valley. The water rose so suddenly that, when the barn doors were opened, the animals had to swim to safety. Vehicles were flooded or swept away and the bridge was wrecked. Three houses on the riverbank were filled to the roof with sand and branches.

The village has still not recovered; the new school has now closed; the health centre is empty; the bridge has not been rebuilt; there is no *bakkal* or *kahve*. A bus runs daily to Serik and from there to Manavgat. There are plans to convert the old school for accommodation for trekkers.

Değirmenözü - Çukurca (5hrs 15mins)

This is a half-day trek to a traditional valley-bottom village. It climbs from the cave up goat-paths and old road to the old graveyard of Yeşilbağ, at the edge of a grassy plain. The village, which once adjoined the graveyard, has moved up the hill - the route climbs via the paved *eşek yolu* / donkey road. After skirting Yeşilbağ, the route descends into a side-valley, crosses a stream and climbs to Çukurca.

Walk from the school to the village *çeşme* and follow a paved path R, between houses to a dirt road. Almost immediately turn R off this onto a paved path which descends to a *kanalet*. Cross this, then the river then climb to a dirt road and wider *kanalet* leading from the cave.

15mins

Continue L towards the cave; as the *kanalet* narrows, turn R onto a path starting under a *çınar*. It climbs steeply then crosses a narrow stream-bed. Climb the far side to meet a wider path and turn R; follow this path NNE/upwards until it levels and crosses an open area, following telegraph posts.

20mins

On the far side, swing R across a ditch and turn up an old road between bushes. This soon continues as wider track then crosses a second open field to continue between scrub to a terraced area with the graveyard trees on the far side. Passing over a narrow path, reach the graveyard fence.

40mins

Follow the graveyard fence, passing over some rocks to a wide green *ova*. Cross it going NNE, gradually approaching the riverbed. Just before a small hill, turn R/E onto a walled path, the *eşek yolu*, which runs around the base of the hill then climbs in cobbled zigzags, passing a house on the L. It crosses a dirt road and continues up more zigzags to reach a dirt road between the houses of Yeşilbağ.

1hr

> **Yeşilbağ** is an extended village on the hillside east of the river. It has a large primary school which educates children from surrounding areas, a few shops and several fish-farms and restaurants. Since it's on the main N-S road, public transport passes through.

Turn L and immediately L again onto a dirt road which runs N and parallel with the main road. Follow this road between houses and fields to a junction with the asphalt and another track below. At a fig tree, turn down onto a track continuing N.

30mins

Follow this track past a house; it soon becomes an old road, in places paved and walled, conturing the hillside with the valley L/below. It runs below the main road towards the hill of Asar Tepe with its flag, passing drinking troughs and a spring on the way. Just before Asar Tepe, it rises to meet the asphalt road.

45mins

Turn R and follow the road to the pass between Asar Tepe and the slopes on the R; just before the road starts to descend, turn L/W with the flag on the L, following a footpath along the edge of the terraces with a drop on the R. Cross an area of limestone pavement and follow a path SW to a gap and the start of a wide goat path descending NW into the valley. The path passes a *harman* / threshing floor edged by a clump of trees and continues less clearly through scrub and rock outcrops to a second *harman*.

35mins

Turn down, just before the harman, to a path descending towards woodland. Under the trees, the path starts to zigzag, then passes a clear path coming from the west. Continue downhill on fainter path, emerge from the forest and descend, still zigzagging, to isolated trees on the streambank. Under the trees, turn R, cross the stream and climb a few metres to the new dirt road above.

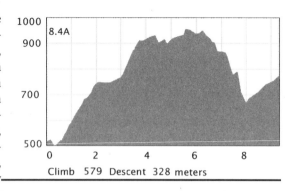

Climb 579 Descent 328 meters

45mins

25mins Turn R on the road and climb up four bends to level agricultural land. Here there may be tunnel work for a new hydro-electric system; continue N to the R bend and cut a corner by crossing a field on old path. Join a village road and continue N/up over a low hill. A paved road descends to the village square and *çeşme*.

Çukurca is a prosperous village of maybe 25 houses along a paved road. The houses are not particularly old, but they are built in a traditional style, with a broad balcony above and store rooms or stables below. It's one of the neatest villages in the area, with well-built walls topped with iron railings along the road, and grapevines hanging over well-kept balconies. The village is surrounded by arable lands, and there are many cows which are driven up the street each morning and evening. A visitor house faces the square; the *muhtar* / headman has a house N of the mosque and can arrange accommodation; the villagers can arrange meals. The village is only 2km from the canyon bottom, where people swim and fish. There is an infrequent bus service to Kesme, 7km up the road, but if a bus is not available, a local taxi service can take you. New hydroelectric work and the ugly zigzag road to Beydili have marred the idyllic landscape.

Çaltepe - Kozdere (9 hrs 35mins)

This long and steep route is one of the most isolated on the trail; although most years during August the villagers harvest the *kekik*, for the rest of the summer hardly anyone lives on the *yayla*s, and in winter the route is snowbound. The forests are in pristine natural condition and quite beautiful. The trail climbs the S side of the hill, continues N on a path running through carstic bowls and meets civilisation at a large *yayla* called Belova. From Belova, the difficult route descends into Kozdere, the steep, well-wooded side valley of the Köprülü Cay. All the route is on footpath.

Leave Çaltepe the way you came in and join the road; after a L bend look for a turn onto the old path heading R/NW for the pass between the two hills above the town. The new road has cut the clear mule path covered with broken stones which zigzags NW/up to a slight pass at Karaardiç/Black Juniper, at 740 m; keep R on the main path.

40mins

Continue upwards passing the graveyard of Hasan Kula Mezarlık on the L; R is a well, with a timber cover and fence, a grape vine and flowers.

35mins

Continue climbing to Yokuşbaşı, at 900m, where you lose sight of Çaltepe below. Pass Sin Sin Kuyu/two wells, one in the centre of a level area by the path, one just below the rocks on the R.

35mins

From here, the narrow path twists and rises between limestone hollows, caused by cave collapses, and slabby outcrops - this is typical of the whole top of the mountain. Pass an oak tree-filled hollow, a possible campsite, where there is a well, Adidi Kuyu, at 1200m. This boarded well is above eye level amongst rocks on the R of the path at the end of the hollow and next to a burned tree.

1hr 5mins

The path approaches a low pass between Hopbilla Tepesi and the main hilltop to a junction where the L turn goes to Yaylabaşı, a huge flat *yayla*. Take the path R/N between small hillocks and ridges to Kesmece Mevkii; R is a ruined hut and L, below the level of the path, another well.

35mins

Just beyond, R of the path is Gavur Kuyusu, a large cistern carved out of the rock and holding dirty water. Cross a wall through a gate leading to an *ova* where goats are corraled; continue N to Kapının Başı, the top of the *ova*, ignoring paths L to Koca Yayla and Elmalı Yaylası, our route continues to a pass where it bears R/NE.

1hr 10mins

Continues slightly downhill through large cedars to a covered, fenced well; bear R/NE to Yalak Mevkii, where 30 wooden houses are spread out around a series of *ova*, although only a few are visible. They have apple and walnut orchards and fenced vegetable gardens and are inhabited from August to October.

25mins

Beyond the *yayla*, the faint path climbs L/N over a ridge towards a conical peak on the horizon. Turn R/NNE across more hollows where there are some huts L, and climb N/up a rocky slope; beyond are thicker cedars and junipers and views of Sarp Dağı beyond.

1hr

Turn R along the ridge passing a hut L then a dry well. Continue NNE passing a hollow on the L to another ridge.

20mins

Descend diagonally NNW/L to a large *ova*; cross it on faint path to another pass then descend past a hollow, over a low ridge and down to Belova.

1hr

Belova /plain on a pass is a large *ova* with Burç Tepe on the L, and a branch of the track leading R/E to Değirmenözü, in the valley below. There are about 20 houses along the side of the *ova*, with gardens, wells and camp sites. It's used seasonally from July to October; the women turn the goats' milk into cheese which is taken down to the village; the men collect *kekik* in season.

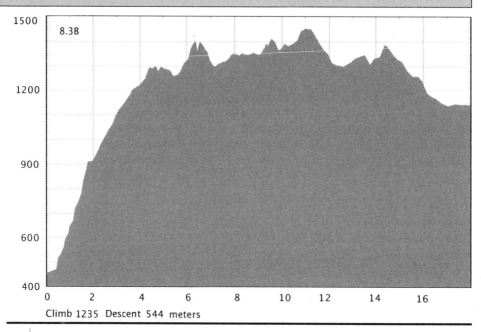

8.3B

Climb 1235 Descent 544 meters

20mins   The main G3 track crosses the *ova* going NNE, and continues descending as good mule path. Down the slope a little, take the lower L/NNW path and cross a stream into tall mature pine forest, some of which has been burned and has fallen. At a ridgetop, at the end of the burned area, turn L/W.

50mins   The path runs on steep hillside with a drop into the side valley on the R, descending gently. It divides to avoid burned trees; take the lower path and meet the upper path again, cross a valley to a wide headland with an old cottage but no water where the village of Kozdere comes into sight.

40mins   The path continues through less dense forest above Sorkun Yayla; a path branches off R/ down to a hut.

50mins   Here the path is damaged by small avalanches but as it approaches the village it descends over zigzags. The final descent to the bulldozed forestry track is over scree.

25mins   Turn L/W and walk with the stream on the R, passing the village of Kozdere to a wide ford over the river. Turn R to the village road.

Kozdere has only about 20 houses, and a steep unsurfaced road which rises in zigzags from the E end of the village to Çimenova, on the plain high above. A track continues W up the stream bed to Pınargözü, but may not be passable. There is no *bakkal* but at the west end of the village is a tiny pension; you can also camp by the stream. A school bus runs in termtime to Çimenova and the driver will offer you a lift.

Kozdere - Çimenova (3hrs 50mins)

The route crosses the side river at Kozdere and climbs up steep old *kaldırım* then follows dirt road to the large village of Çimenova on the plain above and beyond. If you are so tired that you can't face the climb, you can get a lift from a school bus which grinds up the hairpin road to Çimenova.

Walk up the tractor track going NE from Kozdere, to a hairpin and large spring on the R. Turn L/NW on a steep track past a cottage, below the garden wall of a house, then cross the stream. Continue up zigzags and impressive (and difficult) stone steps. Under a large *çınar*, near a wrecked stone bridge, re-cross the stream and climb a slippery zigzag to a stone *yalak* covered by boards.

1hr

The path turns R across a slope then turns L again under a tree. Climb the faint path over terraces to meet the road again.

30mins

Turn L/NW/up on the road to a L bend, and turn R on an old road running from the corner. It climbs NNW over cobbles near the stream bed, over meadows, and below trees, then climbs to the road again.

1hr

Continue to Çimenova, cutting a bend by a well, spread out at the edge of the plain below, and turn L at the second cross roads. Walk down the main street towards a *kahve* and telephone box; the heart of the village.

1hr 5mins

Çimenova / grass plain is named after the large *ova* on which it stands. This is wheat growing country and in summer the plain is a sea of green then gold wheat; it's harvested in July / August. At this busy time of year, villagers from the outlying houses come to harvest their own patches, and the noise and fumes from the tractors and harvesting machines fills the valley.

For the rest of the year, Çimenova is quiet, especially since there are no dogs. In winter it's set in a sea of snow, and the villagers are safely indoors; in spring they scatter to look after new born goats and sheep on distant grazing grounds. However, all the children of the district are educated here, so in termtime buses come and go. There are two *bakkals*, the *kahve* and an undistinguished mosque. The asphalt road leads 10km to Çobanisa and from there 20km to Sütçüler due W; occasional buses run to Sütçüler.

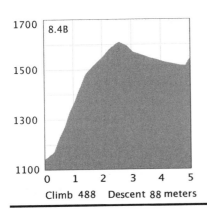

Climb 488   Descent 88 meters

Çimenova – Beydili (3hrs 55mins)

This route is almost as isolated as the last; it's through an area used by villagers harvesting *kekik* or pasturing their goats. The route runs uphill from Çimenova to the southern ridge of Sarp Dağı, the huge bare limestone massif towering NE of the town. It runs along the ridge towards the mountain, and drops E to the tiny *yayla* villages of Gölcük and Beydili. The route follows, as far as is possible, an old cobbled *kaldırım* – probably constructed as a trade route between adjoining Beyliks in Selçuk times. The path is a feat of engineering and the polished cobbles give it a feeling of timeless certainty and intrinsic beauty, but it has been cut by a modern bulldozed road which has destroyed part of it.

20mins — Take the road N and turn R to a tiny *bakkal* in the last house. A good paved mule road rises L/NE across the hillside with a plain on the L, crosses a low pass and rises R around small terraced fields and through stands of cedar forest to meet the new road on a bend.

30mins — Continue E to Arıklı Kuyu, a large boarded well which has good year-round water. Return to the main path and continue up past shepherds' huts on the L, partly following a stream bed, to turn L on the tractor road.

20mins — Walk round a L bend. Continue R on *kaldırım* over an open area towards a craggy limestone ridge scattered with occasional junipers. Meet the road again and walk up one bend.

50mins — Turn R onto the *kaldırım*, climbing in bends and staircases up the ridge to a junction where you keep L/E. The final climb takes you above the tree line on well-paved, wide *kaldırım*, with fabulous views back to the cedar forests and the Çimenova plain, and meets the road again on the pass.

> The pass over the **Sarp Dağ ridge** has a view to the E over all of the Köprülü valley, with waves of ridges beyond, suddenly spread out in front. The air is incredibly clear and, although you can see for miles, there is no sign of civilisation. In evening light, the setting sun floods the ridges and the deep valleys are plunged into darkness. To the left is the bare massif of the peak itself.

40mins — Follow the road R/E/down for 2.5km; the original path is above the road and you may be able to join it for part of the route.

Above Beydili, the old path turns R/down, past a hut then down a valley in zigzags and crosses a low pass then the road again; only 100m further on are the level fields of Gölcük with a few houses on the R.

> The first, old house of **Gölcük** belongs to an elderly couple called Mehmet and Gülizar. It has stone steps leading up to a long balcony and the front door. Here a message is scratched into the timber: *Maşallah yuvasına sığınmış hudasına. Allah sağlık versin.* It was left by three forestry workers who found themselves trapped in a snowstorm on the mountain; they stumbled down to the house, where they found firewood, food and water. In gratitude, they call on Allah to give the owners' health.
> Beyond this house are open meadows with three large wells and a *çeşme*, enclosed walnut and plum orchards and vegetable gardens and a low building used as a mosque.

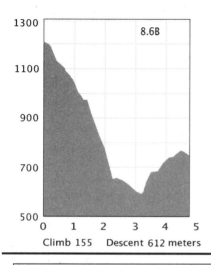

8.6B

Climb 155   Descent 612 meters

Leave the village going SE on G3 path which runs along the valley side with the fields and houses on the L; after the last house, it descends down many small terraced fields then through open woodland and more fields. At a junction keep L, go over a pass and down wide zigzags which soon become *kaldırım*. Continue downhill into the village between houses and head R to the main *çeşme* next to the old school.

Although **Beydili** (once Eski Beydili) is far closer to the villages of the west side of the Köprülü Canyon, Çimenova, once known as Beydili, is its parent village and, especially since their school was shut down, many residents of Beydili overwinter in Çimenova, only returning to their homes in summer. Electricity and telephones are connected and Beydili now has two access roads, although the lower is so steep that most cars cannot use it. In summer traffic on the upper road is considerable.

The houses of Beydili are especially beautiful and use only natural materials - timber and stone. The designs are fairly uniform – a lower stable for the animals, with upper living rooms and balcony reached by a flight of stone stairs; over all deep eaves of a timber-shingled roof. The juniper makes good straight beams and cedar provides the wide shingles for the roof and boards for the doors and floors. The school building is a standard concrete building in a yard; heaven knows how the materials were brought up here. The old school building, of traditional stone and timber, still stands beside the new one, but both have been closed for years. Above them is the village *çeşme*, which incorporates a stone from the Roman hilltop ruins called Asarbaşı a km to the N; they are visible from the highest house.

On some of the balconies are spread felt rugs but, although the villagers have large flocks, these are not of local manufacture and no-one produces carpets any more. The men of the village still go hunting and mind their stock but, by tradition, no-one in the village keeps a dog.

Beydili - Çukurca (2hrs 50mins)

The route continues down the mountainside towards the depths of the Köprülü Canyon, where it crosses the river on a new concrete bridge. It then climbs through fields to the village of Çukurca. Part of the route is on old cobbled path, but parts were recently destroyed by roadbuilding.

25mins

Leave the main village spring on paved track between two houses opposite then descend zigzags past houses to the start of a wide straight *kaldırım* going SE. Follow narrower zigzag path edged with bushes to a pass with an old stone well on the R.

30mins

Below the path is a house and *harman*; the L side is lined with traces of houses and traces of them remain. Continue NE on zigzags, keeping L at a junction and R at a second.

40mins

Continue to cross a stream bed to the R/SE and down a long diagonal over pine needles; you are now surrounded by dense pine forest. Descend to the new road.

40mins

You may be able to cross the new road and use the old path to cut off a bend. The remainder of the path has been destroyed, so walk 2.5km down the new road to the bridge at the bottom of the canyon.

15mins

Cross the bridge and cut a zigzag to the road above. Follow it for about 300m and find the old path on the L. Climb up through woodland on a straight path running E, then zigzagging to a flat area with sculpted boulders and views down into the canyon.

30mins

Bear R between the boulders, then L/NE and descend a winding path, avoiding the hydro-electric works. Enter the village down a cobbled ramp above the mosque, then turn R to the village *çeşme*.

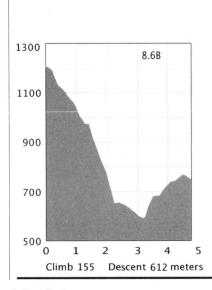

Çukurca - Kesme (2hrs 35mins)

This route follows the course of a Roman road past Asar Tepe to Çukurca. The original bridge over a small canyon is no longer there; according to the *muhtar*, the neighbouring village's camels kept straying over the bridge into the crops, so the Çukurca villagers blew it up! The route involves an initial short scramble followed by a climb up a slabbed staircase. So, although scenic and historical, the initial part is a tough walk.

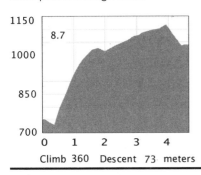

Climb 360   Descent 73   meters

From the spring in Çukurca, walk L/NW on a paved road to the edge of the village. Bear R onto a footpath and cross a field; turn L and wind down between bushes then on a cobbled ramp to the dry bed of a small canyon. Cross the gravelly stream bed and immediately opposite climb up a ramp of loose gravel to a rock face. The bridge that once took the road over this valley is long gone so contour L over the rock face for about 5m, using a narrow ledge and taking careful handholds.   *15mins*

Climb to an old path which zigzags up the rocky bank. Continue climbing N up the steep, carefully constructed staircase, partly in, partly on the bank of a stream bed. At an open area where the old path is damaged, branch R, with the stream on the R, onto a foot path rising through scrub and small trees until it climbs up a bank onto a more open area.   *1hr 20mins*

Turn L/NW onto a faint path which descends between bushes onto a field, rises up a ramp on the R and across a bare rocky slope to turn R on the continuation of the old road. Climb gently through a scrubby area and join a tractor track on a level grassy plain and continue L/NNE on an old road between walls. It leads to a walled area around a few mulberries and a large open well; there are orchards all around here.   *25mins*

Continue NNE up a scrubby slope first on the old road then, where it ends, on a tractor track which bears R/WNW past a well.   *15mins*

The track runs level to a graveyard on the R filled with huge trees, then swings N again to a wide bend; Asar Tepe is on the L/W.   *25mins*

Asar Tepe was a fortified hilltop site from the Hellenistic period. Probably positioned to guard the route down the canyon, the north and west sides are bounded by the Köprülü Canyon and the whole circled by a defensive wall which still stands in places. Inside the walls, the most important building was a temple, which is now totally ruined. There are also four cisterns cut out of bed rock. Outside the wall, on a level area, are two tombs, one in ruins. The other, with carved pitched roof and Ionic columns, stands on a podium. The site was abandoned very early and therefore is worth a diversion.

Follow the undulating road NW, cutting a bend, and continue straight over the hill. Bear R at a junction onto a walled road which rises through a pass between rocks, where the first houses come in sight.   *25mins*

Turn L/down a walled rocky slope to an open area with a few telegraph posts. Take the L/NE road between stone walls (the pension is on the R) to a junction. Turn L to another junction with a *kahve* on the corner; turn R and walk into town on a broad road which passes a graveyard.

25mins

The straggling market town of **Kesme** is about 2km from the canyon and 80km from Isparta. The town, centre of an agricultural district, has several schools, shops and the only petrol station for a long distance; there is a home-stay pension on the approach to the village.

Buses run from the petrol station in Kesme to Eğirdir and Isparta at 6.00am daily except Sundays. There is sometimes a local *dolmuş* down the Köprülü Canyon as far as Yeşilbağ or İkipınar, but they don't run all the way to Beşkonak or Serik.

Kesme - Kasımlar (5hrs 45mins)

This route leaves Kesme going NW on asphalt road, then crosses fields to join tractor roads then an old road which winds between wind-sculpted rock outcrops towards the rim of the canyon. After a few tiny settlements, it turns N and climbs on bare conglomerate rock to cross one pass then passes limestone hollows to a pond and a second pass at Belsarnıç. It descends to the river below, crosses a bridge and climbs to Kasımlar. It's a beautiful route, often on old cobbled path, with sheltered valleys between eroded rocks and spectacular views over to the pale massif of Sarp Dağı, glowing in the morning light and to the hills beyond Kasımlar.

Leave Kesme on an asphalt road running between the graveyard and a large school. The road passes a *yalak* then climbs L around a valley. Take the 2nd track R/W and cut off a loop in the road.

15mins

Turn R onto the dirt road, then only 50m on, at the top of a rise, turn L/SW onto tractor track. This rises over a ridge and ends in a large terraced area; continue diagonally L down the terraces towards a stream bed below. Cross a wall and the stream onto a tractor track and turn L/SW.

15mins

Walk uphill parallel with the stream bed, follow the track to a second stream bed and cross, continuing NW/parallel with this stream. The track swings L/SW and crosses several level fields between strangely shaped rocks. Loose boulders are balanced daintily on rock outcrops and ivy sprouts out of unlikely crevices. Junipers, walnuts and oaks are scattered in the fields. The track swings R/NNW, crosses two more fields following lines of stones, passes a fenced orchard and descends into a neat, straight valley walled by conglomerate cliffs.

35mins

Climb the *kaldırım* from the valley then turn L/W, with a rock wall L and valley on the R. Turn R/up then L with a stone house on the R, between fences and up a narrow valley going NW and onto a wall at the top.

20mins

Turn R/N/up to a path; turn R and climb towards the rounded hilltop ahead. Contour anticlockwise around the hill; the path runs on ledges of the conglomerate rock with a drop on the R. Descend to meet and turn L/N on a path rising from the valley below and follow it to cross a wall between two prominent hills.

30mins

The hill on the R, with a hilltop fort, is called Kulesur/castle wall; the opposite one is Suhasör. Continue on the slope of Suhasör to some ruins on the L of the path and turn R/N across a natural bridge between two hillsides; at the far end, there are two shepherd houses and fenced fruit gardens known as Damla.

20mins

The path continues rising R/NE across a slope then through an area of limestone *çukur /* hollows to a flat hilltop area; this is the highest point.

20mins

Descend ENE into the *çukur* and follow waymarks around the rocks then L/NNE up a rise to a grassy slope, a cattle pond and the final ridge. There are views down through the jumbled rocks nearly as far as the river, and across the canyon towards Tota Yaylası. Kasımlar is just out of sight on the R.

30mins

The path zigzags steeply NW/down, first between rocks, then straight into tall pines with a

40mins	rock wall on the L. Below the trees, turn R/N onto stony path.
15mins	Cross an unsurfaced road, bearing R/NE and turn R at a graveyard wall, following it to a *çeşme*.
20mins	Continue NNW/downhill along a path to the road; after 50m leave it again, pass R of an inhabited house and descend across a field to an unsurfaced road. Turn L, pass a *yalak*, cross the concrete bridge and climb straight to a junction; turn R to a *çeşme*.
45mins	Continue N/up, between trees to a junction then L, following a stream to meet an asphalt road. Turn L and walk 150m on the road; turn R and climb up, following a wall to the top of a field. Climb to a good path through forest with a field below R, then follow track along the forest edge up to a newly bulldozed road.
20mins	Turn R/E past a large school then L/up by a high wall across a slope, up a short stretch of track and up footpath again to climb over a wall onto a road. Turn R and walk up, round a bend and into the town.

Kasımlar is a small town of stone houses with one or two larger concrete buildings around a sloping central square with a fountain. The teahouse (with an old carved door), two shops and buses can be found here. Elsewhere is a mill, bakery and a large middle school serving the whole district. Once the village specialised in goats and sheep and their produce; they are now seen as a menace to the vineyards and wheatfields and so discouraged. Many people have moved away, especially to Kumluca, beyond Antalya, where they work in the greenhouses, only returning home in the summer.

Two asphalt roads serve Kasımlar but the E road will be disrupted by a planned dam. The Tota - Eğirdir road is frequently closed by snow in winter. A bus runs daily from the central square to Eğirdir and Isparta at 6.0 am and returns from Isparta at 1.30 (3.0 on Sundays). A weekly bus runs to Kumluca via Antalya, leaving on Friday morning and returning on Sunday afternoon.

The pension is about 500m above the main square on a bend in the road and close to the start of the walk to Tota Yaylası.

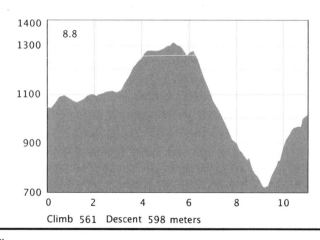

Climb 561 Descent 598 meters

Kasımlar - Tota Yaylası (4hrs 50mins)

The route from Kasımlar to Adada circles the north end of Sarp Dağı. It rises to an open hillside section, then descends into oak forest and passes ruins of an old church. It climbs again to the ridge and follows it, with views on either side, to a junction above Total Yaylası. A steep descent takes you to the forestry buildings. Most of the route is on forest road, but there are pleasant footpaths through forest.

From the pension, turn L on the asphalt and 70m later turn L again onto dirt road; continue to the nearest house then turn R/N and climb the hill to a bend. Turn R between trees to a tractor track; turn L/NW and follow it between a stream and trees to a *çeşme*.   *15mins*

Bear R/N, forking L to a clearer track, to a *yalak* under a mulberry tree; continue NW to an area where scrub starts.   *15mins*

The track swings L/W then S on a walled track around a hilltop dotted with oak trees. Where the track bears L, continue R/upwards along the first wall then a second one, then with the forest to the R and finally into scattered oak trees.   *50mins*

Turns R/WNW/down into open woodland and cross an unsurfaced road; the asphalt road is only 200m below.   *20mins*

Climb NNW/up through scattered trees for 100m to a junction; continue N through trees, climbing gently across the slope to the church ruins.   *15mins*

> The early **Byzantine church**, set amongst walnut trees, may have been built over an earlier building; the doors look strangely positioned. A wall of good quality masonry with arched windows towers over the rubble; it formed the end of the church and part of an adjoining building.

Continue NNW, crossing a wider path, to a gully with a small *pınar* called Sevgipınarı / love spring inside a *çınar*. Walk on level tractor track to a fenced orchard.   *10mins*

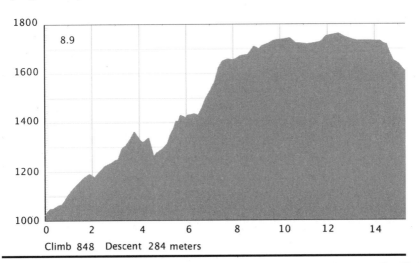

Climb 848   Descent 284 meters

Follow the upper orchard fence then path rising L into the forest, following a line of covers which mark an underground pipe, and cross a dirt track. Continue W on rising path to a second dirt track; turn L/S to the end of the track and bear R/SW/up on faint path zigzagging through mixed forest to an open area; climb to the junction of two wide dirt roads beyond.

25mins

You are now on a high-level forestry road which takes you all the way to Tota Yaylası. Take the upper road and follow it W for 2km through forest to an area where the trees have been felled.

30mins

Continue along the open hillside with views up to the bare ridge on the L and down across the treetops to the valley on the R; some huge pines still remain and there are cedars above. After 2km the felled area ends and the path continues level with open forest above and below the track. After 1.5km, the trees thin and again you have views over the summits to the L.

1hr

Another 2km takes you to a junction. Turn R/NW and soon R again then R/E on wider track which descends, crossing a level track to reach the buildings of Tota Yaylası and the gate of the Forest Park.

50mins

Tota Yaylası is a small forest park on the north slopes of Sarp Dağı, with several monumental trees, mostly pines or juniper. The views, especially towards the Dedegöl Dağları, are incredible and in spring, tiny red tulips bloom in the clearings. The road we arrived on climbs to a forestry look-out building on the very top of the hill, from where the valley, the southern slopes of Dedegöl and the lake are spread out below. Just outside the park is a huge pine, 35m high and 4.5m round the trunk; others near the buildings are of similar size.

L of our track is a small house for the permanent staff of a fire crew and a timber chalet with visitor accommodation. There is a barbecue on the chalet terrace, picnic tables, taps and a grassy area where you could pitch tents. The forestry staff are quite helpful and will point you on the right track.

Tota Yaylası - Adada (5hrs 35mins)

From Tota, the route continues around the end of Sarp Dağı going SW to a *yalak* on a large *yayla*, then due W over a low pass to follow village track to the first houses of Yeniköy. A path rises past the graveyard and up over a ridge to a wide plain where horses graze. In the centre are *yalak*s, and from them a track runs up and over another low pass and down to Adada.

Leave the chalet at Tota Yaylası by a forestry road between the two buildings. Pass through a gate and contour the hillside, keeping R at a junction, passing several small *pınar* and crossing a stream to a junction with a wider track in a valley bottom. *50mins*

Turn L onto graveled forestry road with the stony stream on the L, rising through a plantation. Pass through a gate by a fenced area of young trees on the R and turn R/SW/down on an old track following the line of a buried water pipe through mature pine and juniper forest. *20mins*

Cross an old forest road and descend S through more open forest to a large *yalak* and scattered mulberries; a gravel road is on the R. *40mins*

Turn R/W, cross the road to a huge *ova* surrounded by forest. Cross the centre and enter the juniper forest at a valley, passing a brushwood barrier. After a few metres, the path bears L/SW and turn R on a clearer path on a ridge. *35mins*

Head down the path, which follows a stream bed below well-spaced junipers. Where the slope steepens it swings L/W through some old log huts then returns to the stream and turns R/NW to pass a small stone pen close to the stream and continue down until you can see the yayla in front. *50mins*

At a junction turn R/downhill on a wider path which zigzags to the N side of the *yayla*. Walk for 200m across the *yayla*, past a carob tree, and follow a path into the trees. Reach the *yayla* again and swings R. *20mins*

Follow clear path, ignoring side-paths, just inside the trees to the first house and a *çeşme*. Continue along the houses to a second spring and the asphalt road by the mosque and the headman's office. *30mins*

Yeniköy is a quiet village on the north side of a level plain between juniper and pine woodland on the end of the tarmac road running E from Adada. Another unsurfaced road goes N to join the Kasımlar – Sipahiler road. There are plenty of sheep, goats and cattle, but no cultivated fields. There are a few modern concrete houses but there is no school, no bus and no *bakkal*.

Go R/N on an unsurfaced road lined with old timber houses. By a pylon, turn L/W to open country. Pass the upper corner of the graveyard beyond and continue to two *yalak* on a slope. Curve R/NW up a gully towards the forested hill ahead; cross the ridge keeping just L of the highest point. *40mins*

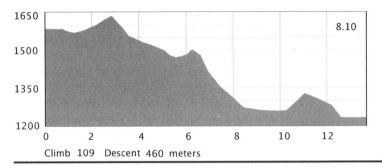

Climb 109   Descent 460 meters

Descend into a broad gully, towards a *çeşme*, where there are a few concrete picnic tables, a triple grave and usually a few horses grazing. Water from this *çeşme* may have been piped to Adada; there are traces of a water system on this side of the city.

15mins

Aim SW for the upper corner of a field marked by a low broken wall. Turn L/W onto a narrow path, which meets a tractor track, and continue along a line of telegraph posts over stony slopes and between scrub and trees to the top of the pass and a road.

20mins

On the far side a path descends a valley to the ruins and joins the Adada - Yeniköy road behind the last temple.

15mins

Adada was built on a plain at 1200m, around a tiny *acropolis* hill. Roads ran S to Sütçüler then through the gorge to Perge; W to Cremna, crossing the Aksu and its tributaries, and N on the east of Lake Eğirdir to Antioch in Pisidia.

The entry into Adada couldn't be more atmospheric. The original Roman road ascends towards the city, cutting a smooth arc through the jumbled juniper scrub of the hillsides. It rises as a line of cut stone blocks placed across the road in a long curve around the hillside into the valley south of the *acropolis*. The stream-bed is below on the R, and as you turn the bend and near the city, above on the L is a *basilica*, which has a *narthex* and an *atrium* with a well. It was constructed of re-used blocks, possibly from a temple; the upper part only is in rough later masonry. It was divided into three aisles by rows of columns; some fragments are in the rubble. On the hilltop opposite, above the scattered graves of the *necropolis*, are the remains of a monastery complex, but overall the quality of the later, Christian building is poor and crude. The road plunges into jungle-like undergrowth on the slope of the *acropolis* hill. On the far side of the hill are rows of seating facing onto a well-paved *agora* measuring 32 by 45m. About 1000 people could sit on these tiered seats and watch performances below. The *agora* was surrounded by *stoa* backed by shops, and on the SW side was once a *nymphaeum*. Mixed in with the scattered blocks is one with a *triskeles* motif, just as on the coins. N of the *agora* was a long thin *basilica*; there is evidence of a *gymnasium* from Severan times, with inscriptions relating to celebrations of Dionysus and Tyche. The next, large building is a 2-storey commercial building, in construction quite similar to the market building at Pednelissos, but of a regular shape. It must have had an external wooden staircase to the door on the second floor. Just past this are several shaped seats, which may have belonged to a *bouleterion* / council chamber. There are no signs of a baths, nor of an aqueduct or even holding tanks for water; maybe they're lost somewhere under the modern road or around the *nymphaeum*.

The largest temple, with a roof and pediment supported by by six Ionic columns, is south of the road. It was erected in honour of a visit by the Emperor Trajan in around 114; an inscribed coin commemorates it. Across the road are two more temples; the E one was on a high podium with steps leading up to the *cella*; it had four columns. A nearly complete inscription dedicated it to Zeus Megistos, Serapis and the Imperial cult; it was built around 200 AD. The final temple also had six Ionic columns and was dedicated to the Imperial cult; it also seems to date from the period of Trajan's visit. The simple and dignified Trajan temples contrast with the rather florid decoration on the later one.

N from the temples and built into the hillside, is a theatre. So little remains that it's difficult to date; there's no sign of later alterations and the stage building has disappeared entirely; presumably it's 1st or 2nd century. Finally, on the route N out of the city, is a monumental tomb, a neat box of dressed stone, some of which was taken to build the local mosque.

The overall impression is of a rich and dignified city, in remarkably complete condition, with no evidence of destruction beyond earthquake damage and the ravages of time. It seems that Paganism and Christianity existed side by side; there's no evidence that the temples were ever deliberately demolished or converted to churches.

Although much of Adada was built after Paul's travels, it must have been a welcome and comfortable halting place on a tough and dangerous journey.

Adada - History

Adada may have been a daughter city of Termessos, a powerful city 15km NW of Antalya. A 2nd century BCE inscription, dating from soon after Selge attacked Pednelissos, has been variously interpreted as a friendship agreement or defence pact or an alliance against Selge or against the kings of Pergamon, who were at that time building a road to Antalya. Either way, it shows that Adada was a substantial independent city at this date; it is mentioned by Artemidoros in the 1st century BCE; later, Ptolemoios and the Byzantine historian Hierocles called the city Odada.

Adada minted its own coins with Zeus Solymeos (a god of Termessos), Hercules and Dionysus on the face; later Artemis Pergia from Perge was added. Motifs on the reverse included a bull's head (symbol of Zeus) and a *triskeles* / three legs (a stone with this symbol can be seen in the *agora*).

The first Roman colonies (Cremna, Sagalassos and Komana) were founded in around 25 BCE; Cremna was close enough to adversely affect Adada's commerce and land-holdings but Adada soon had an impressive array of temples and public buildings.

Adada's bishop was appointed as soon as Christianity became legal. Soon the first pilgrimages to Antioch in Pisidia began; Christians, influenced by St Paul's letters, came to see where this honorary apostle had first preached to the Gentiles. Some probably visited Adada; centuries later the place was known as Karabavlu / Black Paul, or simply Bavlu. According to records of a Church Council, Adada had bishops as late as 787, although they may have been based in Constantinople.

In the 13th century, the Hamidoğlu Turkoman dynasty built at Sütçüler and Eğirdir, but as there is no sign of any new building in Adada it was probably abandoned before then. In 1841, a German explorer Schönborn visited the site, but mis-identified it as Pednelissos. In 1884, another visitor, JRS Sterret, found an inscription referring to games between Adada and Timbriada; Timbriada is about 20 km north. Some research on the temples was done in the late 1960's and the road to Yeniköy was built across the site in the 1970's. At that time, some statues were found under the present-day road and moved to the museum at Isparta. Around this time the mosque at Sağrak was rebuilt using stones from a temple tomb on the site. The site has been newly surveyed by a team from Isparta University but no excavations have taken place.

Adada - Sipahiler (7hrs 25mins)

The route folllows the line of a Roman road from the upper part of the site across the modern road and past a *köşk* / sitting platform. It descends to the wooded banks of the stream and follows it to a rocky gorge. The route through this shallow gorge climbs over rocks and crosses the stream; depending on the water level, you may have to wade through pools. Finally, from a road bridge, it follows the road then farm tracks to the upper/W part of Sipahiler village.

The gorge section is slippery during or after rain; to avoid it, cross the stream at the start of the gorge and follow a tractor track north; where it ends, climb across a field to a wider track and turn R/NE on a dirt road which joins a wider road. This runs N for 3.5km to meet the marked route at the bridge.

Leave the booth at Adada going N past the theatre then a temple-tomb to find a path along the ridge. Turn R/NE and after 200m turn L/N down, following a gully beneath oak trees. It crosses the main road on a bend near a road sign showing the distance to Eğirdir. — *25mins*

Continue down a tractor track, which soon levels out and runs between trees parallel to the main road above. Below an old *köşk*, it crosses a stream bed and continues along the line of a water pipe. Where the path is blocked by brambles, turn L/down through the hedges to a parallel track below and continue to a tractor track on the edge of woodland. — *35mins*

Turn R/N/up and after 100m turn L/N onto a narrower track leading to a ford across the shallow Aksu stream. — *35mins*

Turn R/NE onto a narrow path with the stream on the L, first through scrubby oaks, then across a field, then through woodland to a gully. Here, the path runs slightly uphill and joins an old walled track which runs between trees. — *20mins*

The track ends in meadows sloping down to the stream; continue on path over a dry stream bed and pass below an old walled goat-pen to three unused shepherds' huts on the edge of juniper woodland. A path from the road above to the *mahalle* of Sağlık runs past the huts and across the stream. — *20mins*

If you want to continue through the gorge, head down 100m to the stream bed and the sloping rocks on the R/E bank. Follow the stream N, sometimes crossing on stepping stones; at first you have to pass junipers growing from the rocks, which can catch your rucksack. There are three more difficult places; at the first, climb a short scree slope on the L/W bank and contour over an outcrop before descending to the stream again. At the second, you have to cross the stream by jumping or wading. Just past a large landslip you reach an open grassy clearing followed by a fenced area; an escape path leads R/E past a fence and *pınar* to the road above. — *2hrs 20mins*

At the third difficult place, past a deep pool and a waterfall, climb R and follow a narrow ledge of brittle rock, taking careful handholds. Continue to an old footbridge then take the faint path low on the R side of the stream for more scrambling to the road bridge before Sipahiler. — *2hrs*

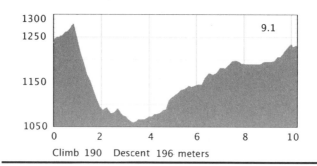

Climb 190   Descent 196 meters

Climb the dirt road up the W bank towards an old *yalak* and follow tractor track on the W riverbank to a footbridge, then a ford and a bridge. Cross to the E side, continuing N to some trees and buildings. Re-cross the stream and turn R/N again to a junction of dirt roads - continue *25mins* NW towards the upper path of the village, joining the old village road by the first houses.

A Sipahi was an Ottoman cavalry officer, who was usually granted a piece of land to maintain himself and a troop for use in times of war. In **Sipahiler** teashop is a photocopy and translation (into modern Turkish) of an Ottoman tax document recording the sums paid by the village in the 1830's, when it had to pay regular taxes. Now it's a scattering of older attractive houses on the old road and a small settlement of battered bungalows along the main asphalt road; the mosque is at the junction. The two are joined by a stream bridge and an unsurfaced road leading past the undistinguished mosque. Opposite it a teahouse and a shop.

Near the mosque is a tiny building with room for two or three people; there is also a room over the mosque. The *muhtar* would love to repair the school for visitors - we are trying to raise funds. The Sütçüler - Isparta bus stops near the mosque about six times per day; it's 30 mins to Sütçüler and an hour to Eğirdir.

There are two routes to Yukarı Gökdere; an indirect one going to a new restaurant on the edge of Kovada Gölü (9.2a, 9.3a) and a direct route through woodland (9.2b). Both routes run west from Sipahiler over a ridge to a *yalak* called Asker Pınar where there are many wild horses; foals and long-legged youngsters are a common sight.

Sipahiler - Kırıntı (4 hr 45 mins)

The route runs due west from Sipahiler over a ridge to a *yalak* called Asker Pınar where the route divides. The south branch turns into a valley and crosses a plain to a forested ridge. With Kovada Gölü in front, it descends past shepherd's houses to a second plain and turns N to descend gently to the head of the lake. It circles the marshes and turns south to Kırıntı; you could continue to the restaurant on the lakeshore or turn into the village. Most of the route is on footpath under trees; the remainder on forest track.

Take the village road SW and bear R at the end of the village. Turn L/NW and cross a stream bed to faint a path which climbs W through low scrub towards the pass ahead. The path follows the edge of pine forest to a wire fence on the pass.

25mins

The concreted *yalak* called Asker Pınarı / Soldier's spring is visible on the far side of a stream bed below. Cross the fence and take the diagonal path R down between young pines to a wider track; turn R and then L to cross a fence then the stream to the *yalak*. This is where the paths diverge.

20mins

Turn S/L for 300m then turn L/SW and follow a footpath on the S bank of a stream above a narrow valley until it reaches a large *ova* partly planted with young pines; ahead is a dry *yalak*.

15mins

Follow forestry track from L of the *yalak* to a junction and turn R/NW. Follow the track to an area of tiny trees and continue NW partly on track, partly following a dry streambed to the NW corner of the *ova*.

30mins

Where the plantation ends, turn L to a path on a grassy bank at the edge of the forest; walk SW up a valley, following a clear path. The wandering path continues WNW through trees to a ridgetop.

20mins

Pass L of larger trees, descending to a small *ova*; cross it to the SW corner and find the distinct old path continuing SW/down, across a small valley towards another *ova*. At the edge of the trees, swing R/NW and follow the path on the L of a stream-bed then through taller trees to an *ova*. It crosses L to a wide ramp which leads to a tractor-track on a large *yayla* below.

35mins

300m to the R are some houses. Turn L/W on the track into a narrow valley, pass a house on the L then cross an *ova* and pass another R to the start of a forestry road descending L. Turn R off the road onto a lower path on the R and follow this steeply down through scrub to the *yayla* below, where there is a well with a boarded cover.

40mins

Turn R and find a wide goat path starting in the NE/lower corner of the *yayla*. Follow it around a stream, across a small clearing, then a second with an old well under a tree; the path is now hardly used and you may have to avoid fallen trees. Kovada Göl is sometimes visible below/L. At the end of a ridge, turn L/W and start to descend more steeply towards the lake; the narrow path continues across the hillside, passing through a rock outcrop and meets the fence and an orchard at the corner of the lake.

1hr 10mins

Cross the fence and turn L to the dirt road; turn R/N and cross a bridge over a canal and a dirt road; continue W to a second junction and turn L/S; at a third junction turn L then R, continuing S.

10mins

Walk S along the lakeshore, passing several turns to a major R turn just before a walled orchard. If you want to go to the lakeside campsite/restaurant in Kovada Gölü National Park, continue S. For Kırıntı village, turn R/W and walk to the second canal, turn L to a bridge and cross it to the asphalt road; turn R for Kırıntı.

20mins

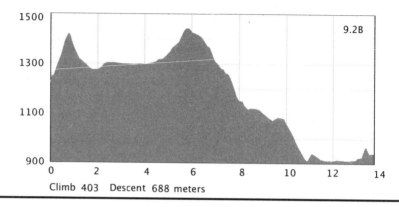

Climb 403   Descent 688 meters

Kırıntı is a farming village on an east-facing slope looking towards Kovada Gölü. Apple-growing and forestry are the main activities. A seasonal restaurant on the main road and a home pension provide accommodation and food. There is a morning and evening bus, a school and a forestry depot but no *bakkal*.

Kovada Gölü National Park

Behind the lakeside restaurant is a peninsula crisscrossed by marked walkways; it has good views of the lake. At the top of the marked walks is a lookout tower and, if you have binoculars, there are views of birds on the lake. The best birdwatching is in the reedbeds to the north end, with black stork and a passage of terns in spring and autumn. The National Park includes most of the woodland around the lake - there are fritillaries, bee orchids and muscari. Inside the National Park, on the lakeside about 2km south of Kırıntı, the National Park services are constructing a large building housing a restaurant and a couple of rooms; there is also a lake-side campsite.

Kırıntı - Yukarı Gökdere (2 hrs)

This short route runs north from Kırıntı village along the lower slope of the hills behind to a valley. It follows an old path through a gap between hills to a farmed plain. From here a tractor track runs to a picnic place, playground and campsite just before Yukarı Gökdere.

From the bridge to the main road, turn R and walk 200m to a field gate; turn L, cross the field and follow path L around an orchard then, approaching the hillside, R to meet the village road by a lamppost. Walk N past the school then to the mosque and continue N, forking L then R past farm buildings to the edge of the village.

25mins

Climb to a newly bulldozed road which runs N along the base of the hill with orchards below/R. Pass behind a cold-store building then between an orchard and woodland. Follow the edge of the woodland NE towards a stream bed, leaving a forestry depot on the R.

30mins

Cross a wire fence and bear L to find a path running along the valley side until you can see fields and orchards below. Turn R/N/down and cross the stream and turn R on a dirt road beyond.

20mins

Walk through trees to another area of orchards; at a junction turn L/NW along the edge of the woods then L/N again on a track through scrubby woods, cross a stream and meet a track. Turn R to a fenced picnic area beneath large trees; pass this and walk 400m, turning R to Yukarı Gökdere.

45mins

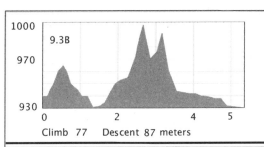

Climb 77   Descent 87 meters

Yukarı Gökdere is a prosperous apple- and peach-growers' village on the east slopes of a high range, part of the Davraz massif. The fruit grows in lush orchards on the valley bottom and, because the trees need very little attention between the pruning season, the men of Yukarı Gökdere have time to collect firewood, hunt, camp out on the summer pastures on top of the ridge, or sit in one of the four teahouses socialising with their friends. The village also has a forestry centre, which maintains Kasnak Forest Park and the surrounding forest and works to reclaim tracts of overgrazed land by planting cedar seedlings. The village won a 'beautiful village' award in 1999, not in recognition of its well-kept beauty, but because it is endowed with advantages – an artificial lake, forests, good farming land and a climate which is comfortable in summer and winter alike.

The two alternative routes meet at the entrance to the village green, where there is a large *yalak*. By a paved square is an adequate shop and *kahve*. At the *mesire yeri* / picnic area, S of the entrance, in season there is a small shop, picnic tables and barbecues and places to camp. A morning minibus goes to Eğirdir (returning about 4 pm); it's also fairly easy to get a lift from the petrol station if you offer to contribute to petrol costs.

9.2b SİPAHİLER - YUKARI GÖKDERE

Sipahiler - Yukarı Gökdere (5hrs 15mins)

The second route takes an old footpath over a limestone ridge into oak forest then follows a tractor track to a series of *ova*, to a third wooded ridge, with views across to Davraz. It descends a zigzag *kaldırım* to Serpil village then crosses orchards to the canal, main road and Yukarı Gökdere. The path is very varied and sometimes rough.

45mins Follow 9.2a to Asker Pınar.

40mins Take the footpath which heads L then R/NW from Asker Pınarı into the valley behind the *yalak*, partly parallel to a tractor track. The rough path climbs through pine and juniper forest to the top of the ridge.

35mins Descend zigzags over rough limestone rocks to a valley filled with oak trees and turn L/ down to rejoin the tractor road. Turn R/NW to a large covered well on the R called Boklıca Kuyusu. Continue on the winding track through pines until the track turns to footpath and turns R/NNE. Aim towards large pines then turn through them to a huge *ova*, Set Ovası, nearly 1km across.

40mins Continue N part-way across the *ova* then turn L/W over a low wooded pass called Alıç Geçidi and down through mature pines, then turn R/N on a faint path. It passes through scrub then turns N and follows winding path on red earth then NW through more trees and descends a rocky path to Alıç Ovası, a small *ova* divided up by fences. Immediately in front are two wells with old wooden covers.

15mins Cross the *ova* diagonally R/N and on the far side find a path rising W through juniper trees, over another low pass and downhill to a tractor track onto another huge *ova*, Kuruca Ova, even bigger than Set Ovası.

50mins Follow a tractor track straight across the plain, with a fence on the L, towards a line of telegraph posts. Turn L/W along the line of posts towards a wooded ridge; take a footpath from the W end of the *ova* to the pass, joining a paved *kaldırım*.

20mins Follow the mule trail down long zigzags towards the mosque and houses of Serpil Köy, an agricultural village next to to the apple-growing plain at the head of Kovada Gölü. The *kaldırım* ends at a children's park and a wide track.

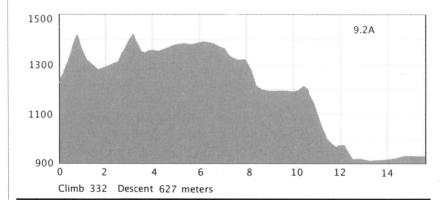

Climb 332 Descent 627 meters

Turn L for 200m to a cultivated field; cross it and take a track to a GSM antenna on a low pass.

15mins

Descend well-used path through low scrub to the level plain and turn L/SW onto tractor track, then the second track R across the orchards a concrete bridge over the *kanal.*

15mins

Cross the bridge then the main Kovada-Eğirdir road past a petrol station and *kahve* at the corner of the Yukarı Gökdere road. Walk 2km up the side road to the village.

40mins

Kasnak Forest Park was created in 1987 with 1300 hectares of forest mainly at around 1600m, but with a maximum altitude of 1848m, mainly to protect naturally occurring oak forest. The huge type specimen of *quercus vulcanica*, the endemic volcanic oak, is the centre-piece of the park. Its age has been estimated as 370 years, rather than the 600 years quoted on the notice on the trunk. It is 33.5m high and has a trunk girth of 7.5m. It's not the only type of oak in the park; there are other species: *quercus robur, petraea* and *cerris*, as well as hornbeam, cedar, elm, ash, two types of maple and two junipers. Some of the cedars rival the oak in size and age. Altogether, 218 different plant species have been identified here. There is somewhat similar oak forest around the routes north of Kovada lake, at a slightly lower altitude and on deeper soil.

In May, the best month for flowers, you will see on the route near Çatal Armut masses of juno irises of a rare multi-coloured variety; yellow tulips and fritillaries flourish nearby. Under the oaks grow masses of *peonia maculata*, a cerise-red single paeony with golden stamens, in company with *lathyrus aurea /* golden pea, and *doronicum*, a tall, yellow daisy.

Bird life is rich; not surprisingly, wrens, flycatchers, tits and nuthatches are common, and three varieties of woodpecker – middle, white backed and greater – have been seen. Wild boars and goats frequent the denser woodland; the mature male boars often reach huge size and weight, but are surprisingly elusive. Other wild animals include foxes, badgers, martens and, the locals claim, wolves.

YUKARI GÖKDERE - BALKIRI

Yukarı Gökdere - Balkırı (5hrs 20 mins)

The route climbs through oak and pine scrub then contours through cedars along the east-facing slope of Davraz to a farmhouse at Balkiri. There are views over the dam above Yukarı Gökdere and as far as Kovada Lake and in season, there are shepherd encampments in many places along the route. You could make a detour into Kasnak Forest Park to see better-managed vegetation - the best season is May-June. The trail runs through oak scrub, on forest tracks along the boundary of the Park and finally on a mixture of trails.

50mins

From the fancy marble *çeşme* at the entrance to Yukarı Gökdere, take the asphalt road NW past the shop then a mosque; turn diagonally R past the old school onto a rough road rising uphill and out of the village, past a bend to a grassy hilltop with a central tree.

50mins

Turn R/N onto a goat path rising from above a tiny quarry into scrub; ignoring a R turn continue across a gully until you are close above a bend on the road below. Find a R/E turn onto a rising path which slips through a gap between rocks then turns L/N along a goat path climbing the hillside. Continue along the top of the ridge, still climbing slightly, to a grassy plain where the path becomes tractor track, going over a low pass. In front is a large *ova* with a dirt road across it.

35mins

Turn R/down and follow good path along the edge of the woods to the E corner. Climb tractor track to a junction; keep L/N and continue, passing an *ova* on your R. Cross a tractor track to a *yayla* and pass a well on your L; rejoin the track and continue N through forest. Continue across another small *ova* and through forest to a much larger one. Walk to the N end; where the track swings R, the route continues L/N.

9.4

Climb 742   Descent 288 meters

45mins

Follow a path N on the L of a valley then swing R and continue to clearer track; it bends L and climbs to a large *ova*. Follow the forest on the L side to the N end. Continue on clearer tractor track going NW into woodland, then climbs parallel to the wide dirt road and joins it on a bend.

This road marks the lower boundary of Kasnak Forest; you are now 300m below and due

E of the monumental oak which is at the heart of the park. Continue only 200m on road then turn R just before a bend and descend to a small *ova*; cross it going NNW and follow path on the far side through oak woods, up a stream valley and rejoin the road on a R bend just before it rises to a huge *yayla*.

25mins

Follow the road along the lower side of the *yayla*; about 1/3 of the way along is a marked path leading up to the oak tree. Continue up bends to a tractor track leading R/N down a valley, across an *ova* and up a steep climb to a large *yayla* crossed by tracks.

30mins

Cross NW to a path leading into forest; it climbs to a ridge then descends quite sharply to a sloping *ova* with the dirt road on the far side. Cross the *ova* and turn R on the road then follow it down for only 200m.

35mins

Turn L/NNE/up onto an old path running parallel with the road; pass above a quarry, contouring away from the road then climbing steeply to a pass above a second, larger quarry. Find the old path again as it descends towards the dirt road and follow this through open country over a low pass and down to a farmhouse on the R.

1hr

Balkiri is the name of the village 5km below in the valley, with apple stores and marble mines on the hillside above and in front; the excavations and heavy lorries, as well as explosions, are despoiling this side of Davraz Dağı. The second house is owned by a retired colonel and his wife; they have a couple of rooms for visitors or you can camp nearby.

Akpınar is a small village with rows of neat houses and a picnic place/restaurant on a hilltop. It has a weekly market and regular bus service to Eğirdir. You can visit Prostanna and climb to the summit of Sivri Dağı (1700m) from Akpınar - it adds 2hrs 45 mins to the trip.
From the road in Akpınar, continue on asphalt and, as the road bends R, turn onto a track going slightly down between hedges. Take the L/upper track and keep L again above the graveyard. At a fork, bear R/N, passing 3 poplars by a *yalak* and continuing to rejoin wider track. Where this swings L, continue up fainter paths to the pylon on the saddle between Sivri and the ridge of Davraz Dağı (1hr 15mins).
Here are the remains of **Prostanna**, a city which may date from before the Hellenistic period; it was certainly abandoned at the end of the Roman period. The earliest inscription mentions the 'people of Prostanna in Pisidia' and honours an officer of the province of Asia in 113 BCE. Coins have been found dating from the 1st century BCE, and from the reign of Antoninus Pius (138-161 AD) to Claudius II.
The *acropolis* was on a low hill SW of Sivri; there were walls on both this hill and on Sivri itself. Between the two hills, under the pylon line, are remains of a *podium* of a temple, fragments of columns and dressed stones. SE, below the wires, are the scant remains of a tiny theatre; you can just make out the line of the seats in the grass. Architectural fragments, an altar and inscriptions are in Isparta Museum.
From Prostanna it's a quick and easy climb to the summit of **Sivri Dağı**. Take the clear path which ascends R/E of the peak, and then swings L/W up the line of an old wall. At the top of the wall you can easily make your way to the summit (30mins). On top is a summit register; you can add your name and comments. In front is what you came for; the view right down on the town of Eğirdir and Green Island, joined by a causeway. The peninsula interrupts the spreading expanse of turquoise which seems to stretch to the sky. The line of clouds on the eastern horizon is in fact the line of summits of Dedegöl Dağı and the Sultan Dağları.
North is Barla, a mound on the northern horizon, above its deeply cut forested valleys. Eğirdir clings to the mountainside below; it's easy to see why it was such a strategic point and so important on the junction of caravan routes running west-east and south-north. Descend to the road the way you came (1hr).

Balkırı - Eğirdir (3hrs 20mins)

This is a pleasant half-day's walk, surprising you with your first views of the beautiful green lake of Eğirdir. It runs through a village with a open-air picnic area and a bus service, so you may decide to have lunch and take a ride down to Eğirdir. If you walk down, the route mainly follows a narrow asphalt road but cuts the bends. From Akpınar, you could climb Sivri Dağı, a neat little Matterhorn of a peak with a dramatic view over the lake.

1hr 30mins

From the farmhouse continue NE, passing a road to a sharp R corner. Turn L/NE on a footpath which climbs the hillside close to the forest and meets road on a hairpin bend. On the bend turn R /NE on a footpath leading up, over a quarry and along the hillside through a gap; where the main path turns R/downhill, continue climbing slightly to another hilltop. Descend wide old road to join the quarry track which leads along the hillside, joins a second track and continues to a 5-way junction.

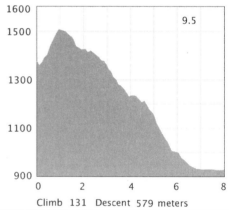

30 mins

Carry on straight across on a tractor track around the base of a hill, descending and cutting a corner on a lower track. Pass through a gate onto a wider dirt road. Turn L and walk into Akpınar, passing over a stream.

1hr 20mins

Eğirdir is 3km below you, down easy asphalt with paths cutting the zigzag bends. At a fork, keep L on the shorter road which emerges onto the main Eğirdir-Konya road just behind the large block of the State Hospital. Turn L again and walk the last few minutes into town.

Eğirdir - History

Early in history, Eğirdir passed from the Hittites to the Phrygians and then to the Lydians. In the 5th century BCE Croesus, king of Lydia, constructed a castle here. The Persian Royal Road from Sardis to Babylon ran across the plain at the head of Lake Hoyran; Eğirdir guarded one of the approaches to the road. Presumably Prostanna was poised on the pass because the lakeshore was marshy and malarial, and because it commands views over the plain to the east. By Byzantine times, settlement had again moved down the hill for it was called Akrotiri / promontory; the population probably subsisted on fishing. After 1071 people moved away in face of the Turkish advance. In 1119 Emperor John Comnenus went on the offensive and re-took the far more important town of Uluborlu / Sozopolis and tried to advance through Eğirdir but was unable to make much progress.

After the battle of Myriocephalon in 1176, the Selçuk advance swept past the lake and raiders penetrated nearly as far as the Aegean coast. Eğirdir's castle was rebuilt by Alaeddin Keykubat 1 and later restored by the Hamidoğulları. There was an inner and outer castle; now only the inner castle remains on a small mound. Keykubat also established a trading *han* opposite the island, just outside the castle walls. The baths date from around the same time, as does the Hızır Bey mosque in the town centre. The mosque, as extended by Hizir Bey in the early 13th century, has wooden pillars supporting the high roof, a simpler, but taller doorway than the *han / medrese* opposite and a wooden porch protecting the doorway. The doors are beautifully carved and of uncertain age. The mosque's minaret is on the wall between the *han* and the mosque; this was originally part of the castle, and the minaret, known as the *kemerli minare /* minaret with an arch, is built above the original castle door.

Felekeddin Dündar, who controlled Uluborlu and the northern lakeland area, took over Eğirdir, now re-named Felekabad, from Alaeddin. He converted the town-centre *han* to the Dündar Bey Medrese, adding an intricately decorated doorway; it's now used as a shopping centre. The capitals with their bird carvings, are Byzantine; the columns Roman. Under Hamid Bey, who succeeded Dündar in 1307, the city grew prosperous. Ibn Battuta visited in 1331/3; he mentions a Dervish convent and the tomb of Baba Sultan, which still stands on the lakeshore near the beach. He also praises Felekabad for its markets, rivers, trees and gardens; at this time it was bigger than Isparta or Burdur. But the Hamidoğulları dynasty became involved in disputes with the Turcomans of Denizli and fifty years later, as the independent principalities collapsed, the Ottomans took over. Eğirdir was no longer so strategically significant – the Byzantines had retreated towards Constantinople and the Crusaders had passed by.

Eğirdir and its district never regained its importance; by 1522 Isparta had 446 households as against 335, including 50 Christian families, in Eğirdir. In 1579 Isparta became the provincial capital, producing wool and opium. The Yoruk population outside the towns was far greater than that within the walls; about 3000 nomad tents were counted around Eğirdir. In the 17th century a character called Katircioğlu, with a rebel gang, raided commercial and official traffic on the roads. Many nomads, who resented Ottoman attempts to collect taxes, supported him. From 1850, to try and control banditry, police posts were constructed along the roads; their protection enabled the towns' population to increase. In the mid-nineteenth century, as the Ottoman government of the time lacked both the technical expertise and finances to undertake such a huge project, the British constructed Turkey's first rail system. The Eğirdir railway was used to ship fish to İstanbul; on the platform at the old-fashioned station building is a Victorian-era weighbridge made by the British firm of H Pooley. Later on the Germans, anxious to draw the Ottoman Empire into their sphere of influence, won railway construction contracts and the names of German manufacturers can be seen on the rails at Eğirdir. The line was probably built around the time of the grandiose Berlin-Baghdad railway project, which bypasses Eğirdir to the east.

The Greeks lived mainly on the island, Nis Adası, now called Yeşil Ada. The three-aisled island church, St Stephen's, dates from the late 14th century and was originally plastered and decorated with frescoes. It's now been partly restored but is still not open to the public. The early years of the republic saw the repatria-tion of the Greek population to mainland Greece, leaving the lovely old wooden houses on the island to decay. Turks from eastern Anatolia were encouraged to move west but they knew little about fishing. The causeway joining the islands to the mainland was constructed from about 1976, and the road completed at the end of the 1980's. Since then, most of the original houses have been demolished and a jumble of pensions have arisen in their place.

The town was an important fishery and Isparta University has a branch dealing with fisheries close to the lakeside. Pike-perch were introduced into the lake in 1955 and soon wiped out most of the native species. They grew to great size and were exported for a number of years; the local crayfish were also exported until 1985, when a plague wiped them out. Since then, the pike-perch have only been caught in smaller sizes and are sold locally, along with the *sazan /* carp, which survived alongside them. The harbour is rarely busy; to get a reasonable catch it's necessary to lay miles of net, a backbreaking job. Apples (mainly golden delicious) are grown on the orchards south of the lake and kept in cold stores for sale off-season. Eğirdir is also a market centre for the local villages; on Thursdays the square and streets are filled with stalls displaying local produce. Since the 1980's Eğirdir has started to attract tourists but many visitors only stay for a day or two en route from Antalya to Cappadocia.

Eğirdir has plenty of places to stay; the pensions on the island, along the 1km causeway, have beautiful views, but the ones in the town are more convenient for the shops. Most have internet and can organise transport around the route. The tourist office is about 1km along the Isparta road and keeps office hours. Visitors can rent bicycles, take daytours to Çandır Canyon or the mountains and swim in the shallow lake. Eğirdir has restaurants everywhere, several banks, a PTT, hardware shops and supermarkets, stalls for fresh fish, fruit and vegetables and shops selling outdoor gear to the commandos and climbers. Market day is Thursday; villagers bring in produce ranging from yoghurt to wooden spoons. The fruit and vegetable section, under the castle walls, is best, but you can buy everything from headscarves to machetes.

The *otogar* is alongside the lake, however through buses often stop on the Konya road opposite the taxi rank. Intercity buses run to Konya, Antalya, İstanbul, Ankara and Cappadocia; local buses run to Yalvaç, Çandır, Sütçüler, Kesme, Kasımlar (see Chapter 4). There are several local buses (blue / white) and *dolmuş*es running from the *otogar*.

Eğirdir / Hoyran Lake has a surface area of 488 sq km, and, at 48km long, N to S, is the fourth largest inland lake in Turkey. It's divided into two separate areas by a neck only 2km across; the northern part is known as Hoyran Gölü. The south section is up to 13m deep, but Hoyran Lake is 4m deep at most and has far more reed beds and vegetation than the main lake. It also has an island, Limenia, which once was walled and had a monastery; it was linked to the mainland by a causeway which was visible until the 1950's and contnued as an old road to Yalvaç. There are no real rivers feeding the lake; the water comes from runoff from the surrounding lands. It's reduced by evaporation and had no outlet until the southern canal was cut. The water level was then raised by about 2m; the level now fluctuates according to the amount used for irrigation and to supply the hydroelectric station at Kovada.

Water temperature can reach 25C in summer and below freezing in winter but the lake has not iced over since 1992. As the *Poyraz* / north wind is channeled down the lake, the weather can be stormy; the lake changes colour according to the prevailing wind and weather, varying from mint green through sparkling turquoise to a forbidding grey. There are several beaches around the lake; the best is at Yazla, the suburb of Eğirdir on the Barla road; it's about 2km from the town centre. The island itself has a small beach next to the small harbour on Yeşil Ada and there are two or three more tiny beaches on the N side of the causeway. The swimming season is reckoned to be June to October.

Eğirdir - Bedre (4hrs 5mins-)

This is a half-day trek from Eğirdir to a small village at the foot of a hill. The route runs along the railway line and over a high, iron viaduct. It's an eerie feeling walking with gaps beneath your feet, but the viaduct offers lovely views of the lake. Isparta – Eğirdir train services have been suspended recently, so it's pretty safe, though not terribly comfortable, to walk on the single railway line. The rest of the route is mainly on dirt track with some footpath.

The route leaves Eğirdir by the railway track to Isparta. From the town centre, walk N along the lakeside and then follow the main road uphill. Just past the entrance to the military camp on the hill, turn R to Barla. Turn L for 200m to the railway station. *45 mins*

Walk N from the station along the line, between fields and a line of apartment blocks fringing the lake, to an iron bridge. Cross the viaduct then, before the bend, turn R/downhill onto a path then track and join the main road below the tourism school. *35 mins*

Walk around a L then a R bend; where the road rises turn L/along a fence for 100m then R/NNE on goat path steeply up a hill, past some pens and down the far side to a pylon. Turn L on the pylon track and contour above the road to meet a dirt road at the edge of orchards. *45 mins*

Turn L and follow the winding road through orchards to asphalt; cross and continue; the track soon climbs the hillside and contours around through scrub then descends again to orchards. Continue as the track bends R then, just past a building turn L and continue NW to a kanalet. Turn R and walk to the asphalt. Turn L and after 100m bear R onto rising dirt road leading straight to Bedre. *2hrs*

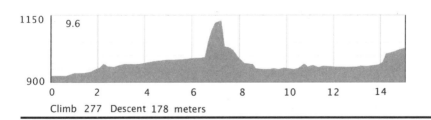

1150   9.6

900

0   2   4   6   8   10   12   14

Climb 277 Descent 178 meters

Beydere (abbreviated to **Bedre**) is a small farming village on the southern slopes of the Barla massif, in spring sitting above a sea of apple blossom. There are two stately old houses on either side of the road into the village; the upper one commands fine views from a *cumba* / bay window, and the lower is of beautiful stone construction, decorated by a painted frieze around the eaves. Two rather neat stone *yalak* and a pleasant mosque on the lower village road complete the impression of grandeur passed away. Unfortunately there is no shop or teahouse; Eğirdir is close enough to supply all needs.

Bedre - Bağören (5hrs 45mins)

This day's walk follows part of the old, partly paved road west of the lake to Isparta. It climbs steeply from Bedre to the ridge on the north, then traverses stony, well-grazed land with scattered junipers. After a low pass it follows a stream valley north-east amidst larger trees. The wider track rises away from the stream to a low pass; Bağören is immediately below in a wide valley sloping east down to the lake. This trek is a venture into a completely different way of life followed by the shepherds who graze these limestone slopes. There are several *yayla*s along the route and in spring you will see lambs; later milking of the ewes and cheese or yoghurt-making. Of course the flocks are guarded by large dogs; try not to surprise them or appear threatening. If they approach too close, pick up and show them a stone and be prepared to throw it.

20mins

From the *çeşme* near the mosque in Bedre, walk NW/up and out of the village. When the dirt road meeets another road, turn R/N/up across a narrower track alongside a large animal pen and find a footpath rising N.

1hr 30mins

Continue upwards then turn L/NW, still climbing on wide goat path; in places traces of the old road are visible. Climb towards a dip in the ridge; as you approach the scrub gets denser and the path swings R/N again and becomes steeper. Close to the ridge, the path runs in a gully between rocks then swings R for the final climb to the top.

25mins

On the ridge, the path is not obvious - walk NE through scattered junipers for 100m to find the faint path running N, becoming clearer as it approaches a stream bed.

1hr

Continue L/NW/up the shallow gully towards a pass; cross a grassy area and the high-point, marked with stone walls, then follow a line of grassy *ova*s. At the end, bear R down a limestone bank and cross a large *ova* to some taller trees and a shepherd's hut at the N end.

50mins

Continue veering slightly R/up through junipers then descend to an *ova* with banks of red soil; turn L/NW and descend across a slope with trees R, joining a wider path. Pass two *yalak*s and continue down to two huge oaks in a dip.

30mins

Pass L of the trees then follow the clear path NW along a very gently slope, gradually approaching a steam-bed below; close to the stream the *kaldırım* becomes visible again.

Cross the dry stream and climb the *kaldırım*, walled in places, as it swings L/N and climbs to a pass just before Bağören. The area at the top of the pass is rough and wide; soon Bağören comes into sight. Descend the dry, stony hillside keeping L of an outcrop to a series of *yalak*s then through fields in the valley-bottom to pass between houses to a stony village road.

1hr

Turn R/NE and climb to the centre of the village. The pension is up a cobbled ramp on the L, past a *çeşme* to the highest house.

10mins

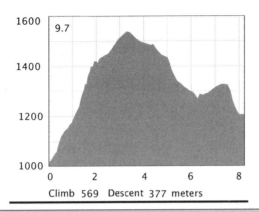

9.7

Climb 569   Descent 377 meters

Bağören is a small village on the east slopes of Barla Dağı overlooking Eğirdir Lake without a shop, bus or school. The stone-and-timber houses all face the same way, south, and have one storey on the upper side but animal pens below the balconied living rooms on the lower side; many have vegetable gardens. Bağören, with its sister village Barla, is the centre of the rose-growing and distilling trade. The slopes above the lakeside are covered with gardens with rows of the sweet-smelling, pink-flowered double İsparta rose, which flowers and is harvested in June. Sacks of petals, brought to the old school on donkey-back, are required to make tiny quantities of the distilled rose oil.

The other local occupation is goat-herding with associated cheese-making. The shepherds move to different *yaylas* during the course of the year to make the best of the poor grazing; in summer the village seems empty. However, near the top of the village is a house belonging to the Lale Pension in Eğirdir; it has not yet been restored but you may be able to make arrangements to stay.

You now have a choice of two routes - the first, 9.8a, is a long walk into the mountains west of the lake, which gives you the opportunity to climb Barla summit - at 2799m one of the triangle of mountains (Davraz, Barla and Dedegöl) which encircle Eğirdir lake. The second, 9.8b follows the Roman road across the canyon direct to Barla village.

Bağören - Barla via Kalkan Geçiti (1800m) (8hrs 45mins)

This is a long trek which describes an almost complete circle west from Bağören village, around Kaymaz Dağı, over Kalkan Geçiti and back to Barla. A quarry and associated tracks on the W end of the Kaymaz massif has created dust and noise and may have damaged a short part of the route. The route, mostly on footpath, starts as a steady but easy climb to the west of Kaymaz, then a steeper climb to the high point at the pass, Kalkan Geçidi, between Kaymaz and Barla. The maximum altitude is 1810m and the wind and precipitation can be harsh, sudden and unforgiving. Kalkan Geçiti is the start point for the climb of Barla Dağı, (also called Gelincik Dağı) (2799m). It takes you one extra day to climb the peak, which is quite easy to navigate and climb, even easier in snow, but there is no path to the summit.

From the summit an easy descent mainly on tractor track along a wide valley leading down to a small dammed lake; well-used but steep village tracks descend to the ravine below the dam and rise again into Barla village. There is plenty of water and *yayla*s en route and the inhabitants may offer you food, but in winter the mountains are uninhabited and snowbound at higher altitudes.

40mins

Follow the village road W out of Bağören; it becomes tractor track then wide path running through scrub on the N bank of a streambed. Follow it L across the stream, passing a *yalak* beneath a willow then some large oaks then rejoin the stream-bed.

20mins

The path now follows the stream-bed in a small valley, running first SW on the L bank to an open area where it continues R/W. The valley is now narrower and scrubby oak trees hang over the path in places; continue climbing to a junction of two streams and choose the stream going L/W/up.

1hr

The path, fainter now, continues to climb to the start of the streambed, a grassy *ova* between low limestone hills. Continue SW across a series of tiny grassy valleys edged with junipers, rising slightly to a low pass. Descend equally gently, passing between trees and keeping an *ova* to the R. Pass a distinctive juniper to a narrow valley and continue the descent in the same direction, following a shallow valley. The path swings slightly S, passing a side-valley and rocky outcrops then turns R out of the stream valley to cross a low hill and descend to cross a deep side-stream bed by a boulder.

50mins

Continue across the slope on the far bank, swinging R/W through stony ground and junipers then contour straight across a slope. On the far side is a shade tree and goat pen from where you can see the hills beyond the valley below. The path descends to a wide, stony stream bed; on the opposite bank, almost hidden by trees, is a large shepherd encampment, Harmanören Yaylası. The route now turns R/NW on the slopes of Kaymaz Dağı, parallel with the stream, towards a pass. Follow a path close to the stream-bed, heading into the massif, with Kaymaz Dağı and the quarry on the R/NE. The path leads up the R bank of the stream and runs NW towards the pass; as it approaches the top it merges with a tractor track.

15mins

Take a stony path R/N downhill into the valley below, aiming at a group of *yalak*s with five willows, a possible campsite.

Optional climb of Barla (2799m) (6.5 hrs return)

You are now at the head of a pass at 1780m where a sidepath leads into the heart of the range. W of you is a wide valley, sloping SW, with a small stream and several *yalaks* marked by stands of willows. A track runs down this valley to Kapıcak village, 5km away, and to Atabey town, a further 6km beyond this. Barla Dağı is N, up a steeply-rising valley which cuts into the range on the N of Kalkan Geçidi. The path to Barla village runs E. On the S side of the pass is a crudely-made tractor track, leading to a cave where *tulum* cheese, compressed into goatskins, is stored on a bed of ice until it reaches maturity.

In these wide upland valleys, vegetation is scarce and only a scattering of junipers grow on the steep slopes. To save the cost and trouble of upkeep, herds of horses are allowed to graze around the passes, with only the occasional stone hut or stand of willows for shelter. It's a wonder that not only do they survive the hard winters, but that the groups nearly always include a foal.

The valleys are also quite good for bird-life; if you camp here you may be woken by flocks of red-fronted serins which come to drink in the early morning. The tiny, dark birds have a bright red spot on their fore-heads, and a distinctive, but faint, twittering call.

After May, these valleys are inhabited by several shepherds from Kapıcak village, either living in the stone huts, or, more frequently, in black tents pitched over a stone base. If you need emergency accommodation, the crude and tiny huts are usually unlocked and often have firewood at the ready. There are several small huts S of the path and another on the climb to Barla. But the best hut, a family home, is at Kocapınar spring on the E side of Kalkan Geçidi.

To climb the peak, the best base camp is in the valley leading up to the summit ridge. From Kalkan Geçidi, find a clear path which runs NW high along the SW facing slope and into the valley which approaches the centre of the range. The path continues up the valley to a level area with springs under Baca Tepe / Chimney Rock, a distinctive outcrop high on the R (40 mins); possible campsites are around the stream on the valley floor. The summit itself is on the NE end of the high ridge on the L, just before it divides and falls away.

Above the campsites, the valley runs SW-NE and you can clearly see a grassy watershed pass about a km to the NE. Walk up to the R of the pass and turn NW towards the base of the main ridge (30 mins). From here there are two possible routes. The first is diagonally SW/up to the main ridge, then turn N along the ridge top to the summit (about 2.5 hrs). There is one tricky rock outcrop on the summit ridge, where, unless it is embanked with snow, or you have the nerves for a scramble, you have to drop down and circle R. The second route is to contour NE for over a km on the slopes of the valley ahead, and at the half-bowl facing you at the end of the valley, turn L/NW; circle below a ridge on the L and climb R/up, until you are over the rock band ringing the bowl. From here, a wide dry gully leads up due W to the summit; you have to zigzag up it over loose stones and scree. From the top of the gully, it's a short climb SW to the summit (3 hrs). This route is not good for a large group, as the leaders may dislodge stones onto the others, but it's an excellent route in snow, when you can kick steps.

From the peak, you can see the other two peaks in our triangle, Davraz to the south, and the Sultan Dağları and Dedegöl stretching towards the southeast. Sivri is also visible, perched above the lake. North-east is the line of the Karakuş Dağları / Blackbird mountains, hemming the north of the lake. Due north is a deep bowl, cut out above the forest, called Ayıyalağı / Bear's water trough. We once saw strange footprints while climbing the peak in winter; too big to be wolf; we like to think they were bear prints and that some still inhabit the mysterious northern cedar forests.

The most impressive sight from Barla Dağı is the lake itself, spread out below, maybe bewitched by ethe-real early morning mist, with the far shore melting in shades of ecru and smoke into the ranges beyond. If you're lucky, not a ripple, not a breath of wind disturbs the tranquil tints of its surface. And all is silence and space (but be warned; both Barla and Davraz are under the flight path of aircraft flying Antalya – İstan-bul, and if you sleep out in the valley, the 4am flight is sure to wake you).

Return by either route; rejoin the trail at Kalkan Geçidi to walk out to Barla.

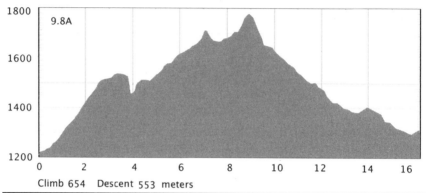

9.8A

Climb 654   Descent 553 meters

1hr 10mins

Turn R onto a tractor track heading NE/uphill towards Kalkan Geçidi, the high pass leading to Barla village. Pass another *yalak* with willows to reach the pass, where there is a stone wall on the R where you can shelter from the wind. From here, you can climb Barla Dağı.

30mins

From Kalkan Geçidi, descend NE on a clear path on the L valley side to the grove of willow trees and *yalak* at Kocapınar.

At **Kocapınar** is a fenced enclosure, a vegetable garden, an outbuilding, a sheep pen and a small, single roomed house. Usually the door is left unlocked all winter, so if you arrive before the family moves up, you could bivouac in this comfortable home. There's a *çeşme* just outside, a fireplace, and enough room to spread out four or five sleeping bags in comfort. From late May to September, Mehmet and his family are in residence with their flock of sheep and goats. Mehmet is just one of many summer residents; all along this valley are occasional houses, usually with a patch of fenced land for crops and a few willows for shade and firewood. Make an effort to communicate with the shepherds; they are lively and helpful and everyone on the mountain is related to everyone else. Remember, if anyone gets lost, or there is an emergency, these shepherds are the best possible help available.

50mins

From the *yalak*, continue into the valley bottom on the main tractor track. Where this divides, turn R/down to the stream bottom and walk E on the old, thistly track, cutting off a few bends, then rejoin the track.

1hr 30mins

Cut another corner, then continue on track to the dam below, passing a quarry R.

50mins

Join the dam road, pass a R junction and continue down a bend.

50mins

Look for waymarks leading to the canyon; you are now on the Bağören-Barla path (9.7B).

If you prefer to walk though meadows and hedges, you could walk cross-country down towards the Bağören - Barla road, passing over a hill and continuing SE to join the Bağören-Barla road close to the graveyard and pass. You can then pick up the route from Bağören and follow it to Barla. (see 9.7B)

Bağören - Barla direct (1hr 45 -mins)

This is a short route along a Roman road which takes you across fields to the small canyon and into Barla village.

From the village centre, take a cobbled ramp past a *çeşme* to the highest building in the village. Continue behind it and along an old hedged road which meets the new unsurfaced road. Turn L and walk along the road, past a graveyard with fragments of Roman columns along the fence.

25mins

150m past the end of the graveyard, turn R off the new road onto the Roman road - at first it is indistinct but it soon runs between hedges, swinging R/NE and contouring the valley side, crossing the stream and meeting an unsurfaced road. Turn L and walk 100m up the road.

30mins

The red roofs and minarets of Barla village are now directly opposite and partly below you. At a marked path, turn R/E and cross the deep valley via an ancient and well-built-up but narrow and steep path, covered with loose stones, which zigzags down to the valley floor. At the bottom, turn L and cross the stream by an old cobbled bridge. Turn L again, then R, and climb a steep cobbled path to an open area in front of a stone and mud-brick house.

35mins

The marked trail continues L/N towards a mosque and overhanging *çınar*, but the village centre and shops are R/E above, reached via an asphalt road or (more directly) by steps and a steep concreted street.

15mins

```
1240
                    9.8B
1200




1100




1060
   0      1.5      3
 Climb 20  Descent 164 meters
```

Barla and its sister village, Bağören, are delightful, decaying remnants of rural life. Both of them occupy the northern slopes of river valleys leading down to the lake; Barla is about 2km further north, and is by far the larger. The old parts command lovely views, for they are high above the lake, but Barla's new development has spilled several km downhill along the modern road towards the lakeside.
The name Barla is derived from Parlais, the Roman settlement which predated the village. Above and NW of Barla, stretched out on the north-facing slopes of the valley, lie the ruins of the Roman settlement strategically positioned to guard the major west-east road across the north end of lake Eğirdir. It's never been

excavated or mapped, and the ruins are pretty vague and undistinguished, but include a massive defensive wall and a rock-cut cave-tomb carved high in the rocks.

Both villages once had a substantial Greek population, which was repatriated in 1923. There is a skeleton of a church, high up the Barla valley; the next section of the route passes it. The main mosque itself was also probably once a church. The Greeks were replaced by Kurds relocated from eastern Anatolia. They were later given the option of returning to their homes so now only a few of the original Kurdish migrants remain; they are very old and have fading memories of their traumatic move. The original houses, with carved wooden fittings, overhanging balconies and enclosed gardens, decay gently and picturesquely in the steep cobbled back-streets; sadly, few have been restored. There are also four massive *çınar*s which overshadow the mosques. These are estimated to be up to 320 years old; the largest is 36m high and has a girth of 7.2m.

Barla is a place of pilgrimage for the followers of Sheikh Nursi. This holy man, born near Bitlis in Eastern Turkey in 1873, was educated by the Naqshabandi Sufi order and acquired a reputation as a scholar and debater. In İstanbul, in 1907, he proposed a Kurdish university to the Sultan, and from then on led the quest for education for his people, first under the Young Turk government and later under Atatürk and the new republic. He was also a military leader (his portrait, that of a dashing hero, with bandoliers, fearsome dagger and beard, appears on many souvenirs) both in the Balkans and against the Russians. According to local sources, during WW1, he was arrested by the Russians while in the Van / Bitlis area. He refused to stand to attention for the Russian officer, saying that his religion didn't allow him to stand for any man. The officer acknowledged his bravery and allowed him some freedom within the prison camp. Maybe because of this, he managed to escape from the Russians.

After the war, even though Atatürk had personally invited him to Ankara, in 1925 he was somehow implicated in the Sheikh Said Kurdish rebellion. For this and for criticising Atatürk's secularism, he was exiled to Barla. The Yokuşbaşı mosque is next to his house and is therefore a place of pilgrimage – in the *çınar* outside the mosque is a platform from which the holy man addressed his followers. Below is a Roman statue base, which he used as a mounting block.

Sheikh Nursi explicitly rejected the old *tarikat* / religious sects, looking instead for a united future. He was buried in the graveyard at Barla but his body was subsequently removed by the authorities, who didn't want it to become a place of pilgrimage. While he was in Barla, his Nurcu movement (Movement of Light) disseminated his collected writings, the Risale-i Nur, throughout the country, but particularly to Kurds. After WW2, the movement thrived and now has a substantial, largely Kurdish following; in fact it's the most important religious movement amongst the Kurds, with its own newspaper and publishing house. The visitors are devout people of all ages, the women dressed in neat headscarves; you may see them emerging from the lower mosque or choosing souvenirs of their visit.

Both Barla and Bağören villages, like others in the area, are know for the cultivation of roses for making rose oil and rose water; the oil, which is extracted from the petals in a factory in the town or others in İsparta, is used to scent everything from cold cream to soap. The villages are surrounded by rose gardens, and in late May you may see the village women picking or loaded donkeys bringing in the sacks for weighing. They prefer to pick after showers, as the weight of the petals is higher; the job is horrible, resulting in scratched and bloody hands, so the oil is worth every penny.

Barla's population is 3000, with 1500 people in the town itself; many have migrated to İstanbul, Isparta and other towns. It's classed as a *kasaba* / town, and has had a town council / Belediye since the 1950's. Facilities include a health centre, and it's divided into 6 local districts under their own headman, with a mayor over them. Barla's social life centres around a tea shop close to the main mosque. There are several other food shops and a bakery in the same street. Souvenir shops for the Sheikh Nursi pilgrims near his shrine.

Barla - Dikmen Çiftliği (9hrs 5mins)

This route climbs NE, up a valley on the E slopes of Barla, passing the church and the Roman settlement, between a rock face and the stream bed to a pass. The indistinct ruins of Parlais are strewn along the route and up the rocky slopes to the skyline. A square opening high in the valley wall leads to a rock-cut grave; there is also a large cave. At the pass, the route turns NW and runs first on open rocky slopes, then through juniper and cedar forests all overlooking the lake. It crosses a valley on the east slopes of Cam Dağı on forest road and eventually descends E across hills, grazing land and through scrub. It meets the main road at the tiny settlement of Dikmen Çiftliği, from where you can take a boat across the lake to Kemerdamları en route for Antioch in Pisidia. The route runs mainly on footpath, first through grazing land then through forest. There are shepherds on the early part of the route and you may see Said Nursi pilgrims around Cam Tepe.

Resume the route near the lowest house in the valley at the bottom of Barla village. Follow the waymarks NW, past the western mosque under a *çınar*, and up the valley. It zigzags steeply up the S bank, partly on old *kaldırım*, partly on dusty goat path, through old and decayed orchards, until it arrives at the ruins of the church. *20mins*

> The square **church** is now closed by a wooden padlocked door, but the two side aisles and open nave are visible through large arched windows. Like the side aisles, the central nave once had a barrel-vaulted roof, maybe supported by columns. There is a tiny apse, which looks as though it has been added later, and a dated stone above it. The area surrounding the church was mainly inhabited by Greek families who were repatriated in 1923; very little remains of their former homes.

Climb diagonally past the church away from the orchards in the valley bottom and find the trace of the old Roman road running parallel with a rock face towards a clump of trees. It dips as it crosses a gully then, right below the cave, climbs L/NNW and becomes much clearer. Soon there are traces of walls and field boundaries then a large tree and *yalak* just beyond. *30mins*

Continue on the old road past more walls; where these end, continue on a goat path which meets the stream bed and a tractor track. Turn L/NW to three willows on a low hilltop then to three more willows then across a wall - the path is clearer now. Continue upwards, closer to the stream, and cross a bulldozed road to a clump of willows with a *yalak*. *1hr 15mins*

Turn R/NW onto a tractor-track, branch R onto faint track then leave the track for a goat path and climb L/N above a goat pen to a pass. The view NW from the pass is over the eastern slopes of Barla Dağı, with rock and scree slopes broken by stream beds and scattered with junipers. Below is a wide, sloping plain, then low ridges running down to the lake. The route runs towards a line of pylons on a ridge clad with junipers. *20mins*

Descend a rocky slope to the first stream bed in the valley bottom, passing two trees on the far bank. Continue across the bare slope, crossing a stream bed with a large tree, more minor gulleys to a wide, stony gully where the path turns upwards again. *45mins*

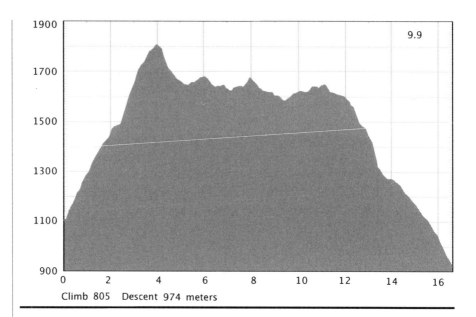

9.9

Climb 805 Descent 974 meters

Continue across more small hollows, pass above a large tree and cross another gravelly stream bed. Meeting a clearer track on the R, continue L/N rising to a pile of rocks and a shepherd's hut. Pass uphill of the rocks, descend across a stream bed and climb to a low ridge. Here, the route is confused, so aim for the pylons on a track which descends the ridge, crosses one stony gully then another then climbs past some goat pens and passes beneath the pylon line.

50mins

Follow bulldozed track through juniper and cedar woodland, keeping R/N at a junction, to a slight rise from where you can see a major forest road ahead, beyond the dark tree-filled valleys below.

25mins

Our track contours L above a deep pine-filled valley to a junction close to the electricty cables. It turns R/NE and descends a chalky, eroded path towards a dry stream bed. Here it turns R/NW and 50m later crosses the stream bed.

40mins

The chalky path climbs R/NE diagonally up the far bank to the top of a hill, then circles L around the hillside to an open area of grassland sloping E. Continue through a few trees and descend a slope to meet a tractor track at a junction. This open area, called Gölet after the seasonal lake which collects after rain, has a tractor track across it - in both directions it descends to the lakeshore. Other forestry maintenance tracks go E.

15mins

Continue on the track going NNE towards cedar forest then round a bend R to a junction with a lower track. On the next bend, turn L/N on a path into young cedar forest. This winds uphill, crosses another track and continues for 300m to a paved road.

20mins

Cam Tepe /Pine hill, where the followers of Sheikh Nursi come to meditate as he did, inspired by views across the lake and mountains, is reached via this paved road. The tree where he meditated is gone, but there is a building near the spot, 2km further up the road. The area is still regarded as sacred, and a steady stream of skull-capped or head-scarved disciples fast and pray here, before visiting a *çeşme* on a large *ova* to break their fast at a special meal.

Climb down the bank and find the descending track opposite; cross a stream and climb the far side through a gate, past a well and around sharp bends for about 2 km, until it ends abruptly. Below are views down to the lake, but there is no obvious way ahead.

50mins

From the end of the track, take a faint goat track across a barbed-wire fence and continue ENE/downhill into a small *ova* with scattered junipers. Continue on faint path steeply down a further level onto a second *ova* below. Cross the lowest part, still heading ENE, and climb over a low ridge and descend onto a third, much larger, *ova*, crossed by a main E-W path.

40mins

Turn R/E on the path then L/NE, leaving some shepherd huts on the L, to the lowest part of the ova where a narrow valley continues. The path follows the valley down, running over rocks and amongst trees. At a side-valley keep R.

20mins

As the descent steepens, the path follows the R/S bank and then circles R around a headland with views over the lake.

20mins

The well-used path continues gently down the ridge and circles L to a second headland where it turns sharply L/NE/down to a level area behind some shepherd huts in the valley below.

1hr 5mins

Descend the path alongside the enclosure fence to a tractor track; follow this down to the road. Immediately ahead is a sign for a fish farm; on the opposite side of the main road is a large farmhouse.

15mins

The boat crossing of Eğirdir Lake takes about half an hour in one of the small fibreglass fishing boats. Mustafa at the fish farm has some accommodation and can of course provide a meal. He will take you across for about 80TL per boat (up to 4 people) and land you on one of the stony beaches close to Kemerdamları. Climb up from the beach to a tractor track running parallel with the shore and turn R into the village; it's not more than a km. It's unwise to cross the lake in a wind, when the waves of the lake are showing white horses; it's not unsafe, but the boats are open and you'll get drenched with spray.

The lake here is almost at its narrowest and shallowest. It's bordered by reed-beds and willows, which shelter a varied and, in winter, vast collection of birds. In summer, coot and reed warblers are the most obvious, the latter from their monotonous calls. On the far side of the lake, diagonally opposite, is the mountain of Kiriş Dağı, which rises sheer from the lake in limestone cliffs and gullies. On the south of Kiriş is a marshy area which supports lush grazing and wonderful bird life; the village of Kemerdamları lies on a slope above the marshland.

Kemerdamları (known as Kemer) has a mosque, an abandoned schoolhouse, a couple of storks nests but no shop. The only bus is the one taking the school children at around 7am to Yeniköy, returning at about 3pm. In other words, access to this little haven is a real problem. If you cross late in the day, you will be allowed to sleep in the school house.

Kemerdamları - Aşağı Tırtar (7hrs 40mins)

This route climbs over the headland of Kemerdamları, then follows pebbly beaches along the shore, climbing around headlands and crossing gullies. It passes over a headland with a cave and descends again to water level then, approaching Aşağı Tırtar village, passes various rock-cut tombs and natural rock arches all arrayed behind a willow-fringed strand. You have the choice of climbing up to the village for the night, or camping on the strand. The route is nearly all over rough footpath; the shepherd dogs near the start of the route can be a menace.

The waymarking starts again at the mosque in the village of Kemerdamları. Follow the dirt road NW, with views over a reed-filled bay and a small fishing settlement on the shore, rising then descending to a shepherds' encampment. *(20mins)*

Continue on the dirt road then on a footpath rising steadily through prickly scrub, about 100m from the lake, to a ridge at 1050m. *(45mins)*

Descend from the ridge towards the lake, turn N on a clear path just above water level and pass over a small waterside ridge. Continue N for 300m to a small ridge coming down to the water. *(35mins)*

Either wade around in the shallow water or scramble over the rocks to the next beach; continue on a waterside track, passing two large *çınar*. Climb around a difficult headland, scrambling on narrow ledges 30-40m above the water. Descend to a beach with a willow tree and some goat-pens behind; in the rocks of the headland, about 50m before the willow, is a source of good clear water. *(55mins)*

Walk along at beach level, scramble across a small ridge and cross a shallow gully to a headland. Then scramble along slabs and head down to a long beach at the foot of a wide gully coming down from the R. Walk along the beach, passing a second gully, several large *çınar* and a stone hut, to some mulberries. *(1hr)*

Just before the mulberries, climb a scree-covered path R/NE then turn L on the cliff edge, bearing N to cross above a cave just visible in the scrub and climb over a low ridge. *(50mins)*

Continue N through scrub and woodland, crossing a gully to a higher ridge with an area of slabby rocks at 1090m. In front are some sharp-edged ridges of rock towers, with glimpses of the lake between them. *(30mins)*

The path divides; continue R/N climbing gently and pass behind a prominent rock and through a gap between rocks. Circle R around the top of a wooded gully to cross another ridge. *(30mins)*

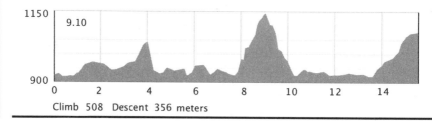

Climb 508 Descent 356 meters

The path descends over loose soil to cross a gully, then crosses a lower ridge below an outcrop.

10mins

A crescent of beach is now visible L/below, but continue N, descending less steeply, crossing a patch of scree to another outcrop. The final descent is over a *kaldırım* down to a grassy slope known as Tek Dut / one mulberry, behind the main pebbly beach. Continue N, just below the natural rock arch ahead.

Continue to a fenced grove of willows then follow the beach NE; just before the headland, 30m above the path, is a rock cut tomb / church.

15mins

Just outside the **church** is Greek graffiti from 1865, inside is a semi-circular apse with traces of a frescoed face, reputed to be that of St Paul, and more graffiti. According to locals, until recently a fresco of a woman astride a donkey or horse could be seen. Immediately after the church is a second rock arch.

Past the headland a tractor track begins; follow it, either on the track or beach for 2.5km, passing orchards and an old cottage. Where the track returns to the lakeside, it passes a fresh water *pınar*; it's a favourite picnic place.

40mins

You could camp on the lakeshore; the alternative is to head on to the village of Aşağı Tırtar. Turn R/SE/up on the dirt road to cross an asphalt road; continue straight uphill with a building L ; join a stony road and climb to a junction with the asphalt; continue R into Aşağı Tırtar.

35mins

Tırtar was once a lakeside fishing village. In the 1890's, sickened by recurring malaria, the population moved up the hill to two new villages called lower and higher Tırtar; Aşağı Tırtar is the lower one. This friendly fishing and agricultural village is tucked in a sheltered corner on the slopes above the lake. It has two shops, a *kahve* and a school with 24 lively children. It's reasonably well served by early-morning buses to Yalvaç at 6.30am, returning at 2.30pm.

9.11 AŞAĞI TIRTAR - SÜCÜLLÜ

Aşağı Tırtar - Yukarı Tırtar, Eyüpler and Sücüllü (9hrs 10mins)

The route circles the foot of Kiriş Dağı to the village of Yukarı Tırtar, then takes the old Pazar Yolu / market road which ran from the old village on the lake to Yalvaç; it may be the remains of the road from the Byzantine monastery on the island in Hoyran Gölü to Yalvaç. The route goes through fields, over steppe, over a pass between Kiriş and Kızıl Dağı, and then east through sparse oak forest and across agricultural land to Eyüpler, an old town nestling in a valley. Sücüllü is a larger town on the far side of rolling ridges of farmland; the walk is over easy farm track.

1hr 20mins

From the old school in Aşağı Tırtar, follow the narrow asphalt road through agricultural land scattered with pear trees 5km NE to Yukarı Tırtar; you may be offered a lift. Where the road climbs steeply towards the village, take the L fork and walk up on track, past the school to the centre.

30mins

Continue NE to meet, but not join, the main asphalt at the last house and a *yalak* just outside the village. Continue on the same line NE/ level on a wide unused road to a fork where you keep R.

15mins

Follow tractor track past a R turn, past woodland and orchards, and rejoin the main road near a *yalak*.

25mins

Continue R/NE for 300m and bear L onto the start of the walled and partly paved Pazar Yolu, which runs below the unsurfaced road. On a bend rejoin the new road for only 50m then return to the Pazar Yolu to the last cultivated field.

50mins

Keep straight on/ENE on footpath along a single line of stones dotted with bushes, keeping R/ESE at a fork to cross a gully. The old path continues parallel and below the new road, passing a cultivated field on the L then turning R to rejoin the asphalt just before a cutting on the pass.

20mins

Walk 200m on the new road and then, before the R bend, turn L/NE to the first oak trees. The Pazar Yolu runs steeply down into a valley then bears R/E and passes 50m L of a red brick farm building, along a field boundary.

1hr 10mins

It passes through a patch of oaks to meet a tractor track and continues through fields, passing an isolated concrete house with a *yalak*.

Fork L/ESE on a grassy track between bushes; cross a stream and pass a *yalak* under poplars, continuing L/ENE around the hillside, over a couple of gullies and a bulldozed area to a bend

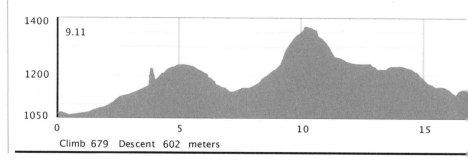

9.11

Climb 679   Descent 602   meters

where can see the village of Eyüpler nestling in the valley below. *40mins*

Descend and meet the asphalt road; turn L/down and continue into the upper part of the village. Walk down the hill past the school then turn L and R/downhill into the main street. The *kahve* is ahead opposite the new mosque, and a market is on the L. *30mins*

Eyüpler is a large village which, like Barla, is gradually creeping down the valley. It has primary and middle schools, a cosy *kahve* opposite the mosque and a couple of shops. The houses are mud brick and timber constructions on stone bases and the old mosque was made by Greek craftsmen. It's kept green by the graveyard just north of the centre. There is a scattering of Roman relics, built into the houses or incorporated into public fountains. On the way in, by a tiled *çeşme,* is a monument to a centurion of the Vth legion, with *Q.MANNAFO.P.F.SER.CENTURIONI.LEG.V.G.COHOR.HSII.HAST.P* inscribed on it. Below the town, on the R bank of the stream are said to be the ruins of a Byzantine church – only the crypt remains.

Locals refer to the village as Ayıplar, which means 'shameful', but if you use the same pronunciation, they soon reprimand you!

*Dolmuş*es run frequently from the teahouse to Yalvaç. There's nowhere to stay in the village, and nowhere pleasant to camp either; the best camps are either by the poplars and spring before you reach Eyüpler, or in the woodland beyond the graveyard.

From the teahouse in Eyüpler, walk down past the mosque and turn L/E/uphill with the graveyard on the L. Continue L/E on unsurfaced road to a small pool at the head of a shallow valley on the R; the church is down the valley on the R bank. *15mins*

Fork L/NE on tractor track with orchards R and fields L, ignoring side-turns and bending NW. Swing R around a muddy pond onto narrow tree-lined track going E; at a junction turn L/NE onto track through open fields. *30mins*

After a stream, the path rises and turns N; just before the village of Yükarı fork R to the upper village road. Turn L and immediately R onto unsurfced road running between houses. *40mins*

Yukarı, a small village on the main Uluborlu-Yalvaç road, had a communal bread oven and old houses on a slope above a stream. Since it's on the line of the old Roman road, it's probably an ancient settlement, but there is no special evidence of this.

Walk NE, keeping R/down-hill to the last houses then cross a field to the unsurfaced road; turn R, cross a bridge and then the main road. *10mins*

Climb the wide track opposite going N along a ridge and, at a fork, keep R/NNE/level. Continue level then descend slightly to a *yalak*, clumps of oaks and a cross-roads. *35mins*

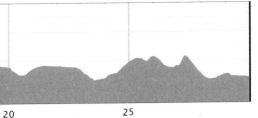

20   25

Above/L is the *höyük* called **Tilki Höyük**, an old settlement mound of very early date, scattered with pottery fragments. You can just make out traces of a ditch circling the hill.

40mins

Continue N past Tikli Höyük and take the next R turn on a tractor road which descends across the head of a dam to meet a minor road.

Turn R then 200m later fork L/E on a tractor track which climbs over a hill, where Sücüllü becomes visible, to a T junction. Turn L, cross a stream and continue towards the town, passing another *çeşme*, Şirin Çeşme. On the top is scratched *suyundan içmeden geçme* / Don't pass without drinking some water. Walk into town between poplars, over a bridge next to a *yurt* / school dormitory, across an asphalt road and uphill through battered old mud-brick houses to the old mosque. Turn R/SE, an asphalt road runs R downhill to a main square and town centre.

40mins

Sücüllü is a *belediye*, with a mayor and Belediye offices above a *kahve* in the main square. You enter town through the older part, with characterful mud-brick houses and a boom-operated well, with a stone counterweight on the long arm. The old mosque has just been rebuilt, and in front is a disorganised collection of Roman stones, column drums and marble fragments. The main square has a stream running down the centre, and combines the functions of communal tea gardens, shopping plaza, market place (Sundays) and bus stop; the road to Yalvaç, with frequent buses, leads S. The Belediye has a visitors' house with comfortable bedrooms.

Yalvaç - History

Yalvaç was founded by the Hamidoğlu Beyliği, a Turcoman clan, in the 14th century, and replaced the abandoned ruins of Antioch. The Devlethan mosque is the most important public building constructed by the Hamidoğulları. It incorporates many stones from the ruins at Antioch in Pisidia in its walls; the single brick minaret occupies the northeast corner. The *mihrab* and *minber* are rather plain and probably aren't the originals.

Alongside the Devlethan mosque is an ancient *çınar*, its heavily drooping branches supported by telegraph poles. Under this tree is the *kahve* which is the old, slow-beating heart of the town. The tree is huge – a notice on it lists its measurements as 10.25 m girth, 3.26m trunk diameter and a height of 16m. The longest branch is 15.8m. It is claimed to be 1200 years old but a more reasonable estimate is 330 years. Yalvaç soon passed into the hands of the Ottomans and acquired civil buildings including a *hamam*, a *kervanseray / han* and a new mosque. Local trades were leatherwork and felt-making, based on local livestock production, saddle-making and ironwork. Yalvaç has in the last few years achieved importance and even notoriety through the personality of the Mayor, Tekin Bayram, a universally respected figure known for his lively and dominant personality.

He is determinedly raising Yalvaç from a sleepy *kerpiç* / mud-brick hamlet to its new role – an international tourist destination. By creating a commercial heart on which the Belediye gathers rents, he has both transformed the town and provided a source of income for future development.

Hotels and restaurants are in place, parks have been laid out, the site entrance and surroundings are neatly landscaped and the traffic system works. The Mayor has not thrown out the old to create the new – the most attractive of the old districts are being saved by the restoration of the traditional timber and *kerpiç* buildings.

Sücüllü - Yalvaç (4hrs 30mins)

Past Sücüllü, the walk continues on track to join the aqueduct which fed the city of Antioch in Pisidia. In summer, with larks above and corn buntings jingling in the scattered bushes, this path is a delight. By walking into the site and Yalvaç via the aqueduct, you enter the city as St Paul did – on a Roman road.

From the town square, walk over the bridge and SE out of town on the road, between a mixture of modern and *kerpiç* houses. At a crossroads by the graveyard, turn L/SE then 100m further on fork L and pass a farmhouse on the L. *15mins*

The tractor track crosses rolling fields, passing a well on the R, to two unusual graves surrounded by wrought iron railings on the L; these appear to be the graves of *Gazis* / heroes; intriguingly, they are undated. The track then rises to a pass. *1hr 20mins*

Take a short cut L/SE/downhill towards a dry river valley which separates Sücüllü from Antioch. Rejoin the tractor track which winds through acacia trees and crosses the stream bed; on the far side turn L/SE/up to a junction with a windlass well on the corner. *30mins*

Turn L/E/downhill, on track through young pine forest, passing over a dry stream bed then turning L then R to a dry *çeşme*, Tiki Çeşmesi, on a junction. Ignoring the other branches, 50m past the *çeşme*, at a T junction turn L/SE level onto a ridge-top track which leads towards the aqueduct ahead; you will glimpse it through the trees. *45mins*

Continue almost level, with some traces of the aqueduct appearing in the path at your feet. On the left is a dam and small lake; the path skirts the Belediye rubbish dump, which is in the process of being flattened and landscaped, with the historic site ahead. *30mins*

Continue alongside the aqueduct, now rising on double arches over a dip, to the wire fence around the main site. The aqueduct rises as a siphonic system to the *nymphaeum* and baths on the hill ahead; you have to stay outside the wire. Skirt the city walls to the main gate, passing a bee-eater colony in the mud banks below the city walls on the L. *50mins*

At the ticket booth are a few cafes and souvenir shops, a pleasant area to relax and leave your rucksack while you explore the site. The town centre is about 1km SSW/downhill; from the site entrance, walk over the junction then keep L at the fork and continue straight to the town centre. *20mins*

We hope that at the end of your trek you have time to spend a day or two enjoying the museum, atmosphere and surroundings at Yalvaç. Finally you might like one last excursion, which will give you a bird's eye view of part of the route.

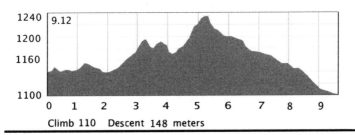

Climb 110   Descent 148 meters

The aqueduct of **Antioch in Pisidia** covered a distance of 10 km from 1465m altitude, giving a fall of 287m in 10 km, or 2.9%; a gradual gradient compared with others of the period (1st century AD). It consists of a steep section descending from its source at the *pınar*s in the Sucikan Dere, then an underground tunnel leading to two bridges over valley heads, more tunnels along the ridge, then the 2km of arches which are visible along the route, then a 800m siphonic section leading up to the *nymphaeum*. A few blocks of the siphon are lying around; more are re-used in buildings in Yalvaç. It's been calculated that the siphon could deliver 3,000 cubic m daily, and it probably survived until brought down by an earthquake in the 6th century, for repairs are visible in some parts.

The main gate of the city is in the W wall and connects with the Decumanus Maximus, the main street running W-E across the site. The *propylon* has been excavated and the fragments are lying on each side of the road ready to be reassembled. The blocks with the inscriptions (inner and outer sides) have been assembled and interpreted by Dr Byrne to read that the gate was dedicated to the Emperor Hadrian by Caius Julius Asper Pansinianus, who was Mayor when Hadrian made a tour of the provinces. Weapons, victories and garlands on the gate were very suitable for a military *colonia* and designed to impress potential troublemakers. Just above the gate is a small area of trees with some tables and a tap, which provides a shady corner for a picnic.

Walking uphill on the wide, slabbed road, you can still see a central water channel running down from basin to basin. The theatre is on the left; the remains are not very impressive, but it was once comparable with the theatre at Aspendos, seating 12,000 people. It was probably originally Greek but was later extended over the road; nothing remains of the stage building. To avoid diverting the road, a 5m wide road tunnel was formed under the extension; the entrance to the theatre was under the tunnel and a three arched gate dated about 313 AD marked its west side. It's possible that a new *agora* W of the theatre was built at this time. Past the theatre, the road joins the Cardo Maximus, which ran more or less level from N to S, ending at the *nymphaeum* and probably another city gate. The street was lined with shops and porticos, which have been revealed by excavation. If you turn R part way along the street, you enter the Tiberius Platea, an oblong area bordered with shops and *stoa*. A notice regulating the hoarding of grain was found here and is now in Afyon museum. This area was exposed in 1924 excavations and unfortunately the locals subsequently helped themselves to the stones to rebuild roads and houses in Yalvaç. But one inscription remains on a large and heavy block; it records that one Baebius Asiaticus paid for paving 3000 feet of the street; this is the combined length of the Decumanus, the Cardo and the Tiberius *platea*. On the R side of the street was a small circular building with a pitched stone roof carved to look like tiles and much decorated; it dates from the reign of Caracalla, who died in 217AD.

The *propylon* on the E end of this area divided the commercial heart of the city from the ceremonial, and is positioned majestically on a rising staircase; practically nothing remains. It had pressurised fountains in front of the pillars; the stone water conduit can be seen. The arch was dedicated to Augustus, Consul for the 13th time, Tribune for the 22nd time, Emperor for the 14th time and father of the country. The last gives a clue to the date; it was in 2 BCE that Augustus assumed the title *Pater Patriae*. On the gate were many vivid depictions of Augustus' victories by sea and land, including battleships and sea creatures, captives in chains and weapons. Probably on the inner face of the arches was a copy of the *Res Gestae*, the first and greatest emperor's final statement to the people of his empire; over 100 fragments of the text are in the museum. There is another copy on the walls of the Imperial temple in Ankara.

Above the *propylon* is a square measuring 83 by 66m, once flanked by *stoa*. On the far side is the ruin of a temple, comparatively small in plan, but with steep rising steps and 8m high Corinthian columns, which made it tower over the surrounding curved two-storey *stoa*, excavated out of bed rock. Not much remains of the *stoa* except the lively frieze of bulls decorated for sacrifice with garlands and fruit. The bedrock with its holes for the beams of the upper storey graphically shows the scale of the building. It was once fronted with Doric columns at ground level and Ionic on the storey above, which was reached by a staircase on the N end.

Before you return to the main road, wander around in the long grass above the temple; there are many lovely moorland birds, especially wheatears, shrike, bunting and larks. If you now return to the *Cardo Maximus*, on the far side you'll see the sketchy remains of the church of St Bassus. Very little has been unearthed, and even the ground plan is vague; St Bassus himself has passed into obscurity.

From the *nymphaeum*, you can look over the line of the walls to the aqueduct and the remains of the siphonic system which delivered water to the city from the far away Sultan Dağları. Owls nest in the steep banks on this side of the site. The *nymphaeum* must have had a raised tank to enable water to be distributed under pressure throughout the city; the required height was about 9m. Below the *nymphaeum*, right on the NW corner of the city walls, were the main baths; you cross what was a *palaestra /* exercise yard, to approach the baths from above. What now remains is mostly the lower or service storey, containing the timber stores, furnaces and heating system, although one room with a *hypocaust* is visible. The building has an immensely strong structure and possibly was partly incorporated into the city wall. In that case, the N door was for fetching timber from outside the city. As yet there is no plan of the baths and there is more excavation to do before the function of each area is clear.

Returning towards the lower gate, you pass the Great Basilica, or church of St Paul. This is a 4th century church reputedly built over the foundations of the synagogue where St Paul preached to the Jews on his arrival at Antioch. Certainly there seem to be courses of older stone below the neat dressed ashlar. From a detailed plan of the mosaics in the main aisle, we know that the building was enlarged soon after it was built, to give the present massive size of 70m x 27m. In the final form it had a double *narthex* divided by a row of columns, then three doors to the main body of the church, which had three parallel aisles, probably with a raised roof over the central aisle. There were additional doors on each side and a rounded apse at the SE end. Bishop Optimus, who represented Antioch at the council of Constantinople in 381, had his name added to the mosaic; we can assume the church was constructed before then, making it one of the earliest and grandest churches in Anatolia. The church has been named from an altar found in Yalvaç with the inscription Agios Paulus; there's also a font dedicated to St Paul in the museum. Around the church were buildings including a baptistery and accommodation for the bishop.

Passing out of the city gate, below is a garden with souvenir shops and a cafe; behind this the city walls and adjacent buildings have been excavated. The foundations are stone but it appears there was a brick superstructure here. There's no clear plan at the moment.

If you walk back to the aqueduct past the line of bee-eater colony, on the left is the faint outline of a stadium in the grass of the field. Practically nothing remains above ground level; these must have been the easiest stones to remove and reuse to build the city of Yalvaç.

Antioch in Pisidia – history

Antioch was a Pisidia city, established on the productive land lying along the southern slopes of Sultan Dağları, on an undulating plateau above the Anthius river / Yalvaç Çay, at an altitude of 1250m. The E, S and N slopes are quite steep, so the main access was from the W. The city land stretched from the Karakuş Dağları in the N to Gelendost in the SE, a total of 1700 sq km. The population of this land in Roman times was probably 75,000 – 100,000; probably 10% of the rural population lived in the city itself, giving a city civil population of 7500 – 10,000, plus a garrison.

The Seleucid main roads ran Apamaea – Apollonia – Antioch – Lycaonia · Cilicia, and Polybios (220BCE) shows how the road was used in the campaign of Achaeus against Antiochus II. In Roman Imperial times, the Via Sebaste ran from the Aegean via Apollonia, with a branch to the coast at Attalia, and continued past Antioch to Neapolis, further SE along the slopes of the Sultan Dağları then to Iconium / Konya.

FVJ Arundell, the chaplain for the British community at İzmir, published his 'Discoveries in Asia Minor' in 1834; in it he identifies Antioch in Pisidia and describes the ruins quite accurately. Then, as today, the aqueduct was the most impressive sight; 21 arches were standing (there are 19 today). Alexandre de Laborde, a French explorer, painted two views of the site in 1826-7, but his son didn't publish them until much later so he obtained no credit for the first discovery.

In 1842, WJ Hamilton visited the site but, in deference to Arundell's description, gave no more that a cursory mention in his book *Researches in Asia Minor, Pontus and Armenia*. Otto Richter, who didn't actually see the site, and JRS Sterret published some inscriptions in 1888. The religious historian WM Ramsay first wrote about the city in 1907, and, in 1911, with a party of amateurs, he discovered and dug haphazardly in the sanctuary of Men.

The first excavations of the city were made by David Robinson and Ramsay in 1924; the Kelsey Museum at Michigan University has some exhibits. In 1984, Stephen Mitchell and Marc Waelkens reviewed the site in their book *Pisidian Antioch*, and excavations commenced under the then museum director Prof. Mehmet Taşlıalan. Now excavations continue under Mehmet Özhanlı from Süleyman Demirel University, Isparta. He has been digging for 5 years and has unearthed late period villas in good condition with a chapel and graves.

Antioch was a Seleucid colony just like its neighbours Apollonia (which had a cult of Seleucus Nicator), Philomelium and Neapolis. It may have founded been earlier but was expanded by Seleucus I or his son Antiochos and, according to Strabo, new settlers came from Magnesia on the Maeander.; Some of the new settlers were Jewish; others brought their own moon goddess cult with them. The temple of Men Askaenos, on a neighbouring hill, dates to the 2nd century BCE, when we know it controlled a large area of farmland and the slaves required to work it. The first coins date from around 150 BCE.

Sometime between 39 and 36 BCE, prompted by the Romans, Amyntas took control of Antioch; after his death, in 25 BCE, Antioch became a Roman colony with the name Colonia Caesarea Augusta. The 7th Legion was stationed in the vicinity and veterans of the 5th and 7th legions were granted land. Citizens were divided into *colonae* / new colonisers and *incolae* / local people, who had inferior status. Later, the descendents of the colonisers went on to win powerful positions in the Roman auxiliary armies serving in Britain, Egypt, Gaul; some became senators. Its most famous citizen was Sergius Paullus, the proconsul of Cyprus, who Paul converted to Christianity and who eventually became a consul. Later the city adopted the title of *Socia Romanorum* – a loyal ally of Rome.

The wealthiest period of the city was immediately after its establishment as a colony; it's noticeable how the original Greek city was buried in a flood of rebuilding. The city constitution was adapted from the Greek original; a city assembly, the *boule / ordu /* council still met, magistrates were appointed in the Roman fashion, but there remained officials with Greek titles. Latin became the official language but Greek was widely spoken and used for non-official inscriptions. Latin is used on coins until the reign of Claudius II (268- 270 AD); the city hung onto the status of Colonia for more than two hundred years.

In the late 3rd century there was severe restlessness and rebellion in Pisidia, culminating in a siege of Cremna; the Emperor Probus attempted to restore normality and Emperor Claudius II brought in new settlers. At the end of 3rd century, Antioch became the *metropolis* / chief religious and civil city of the enlarged state of Pisidia. From Byzantine records, and from the church building, one can see that Antioch was still important in the 4th and 5th centuries.

The earthquakes of 518 and 529, which brought down many buildings in Sagalassos, may have directly affected Antioch; we have no way of knowing where the epicentre was. The plague which, from 543, followed the earthquakes, spread around the Mediterranean, having disastrous effects on the urban population, who were more easily infected than isolated communities such as monasteries or farms. Some cities lost as much as 50% of their population; the effect on Antioch is unknown, but it's quite possible that the population was reduced to such an extent that they found it difficult to defend the city. In rural areas large livestock ranches, which required far less manpower than cereal production, were established; the animals could also be moved to safety away from raiders.

By 615 the threat of Persian invasion was causing further political instability and local insurrections. When, in the mid 7th century, Moslem armies irrupted into Asia Minor, Antioch found itself on the annual invasion route.

Moslem victories stimulated the religious controversy of iconoclasm. Superstitious people interpreted their military success as a reward from God for rejecting all human and religious imagery; Christian soldiers began tearing down the icons and painting over frescos which adorned Byzantine churches. The movement lasted almost a century; during that time Antioch was besieged four times. The Jews, pressurised to convert to Christianity, probably mostly have left.

The siege of 713 marked the end of the city; a remnant population remained but city government and defence ended and many citizens scattered into the countryside or were taken in slavery. In the 13th century, a new Selçuk city was founded further down the hill, using building materials provided by the old city.

The temple of **Men Askaenos** is on the hill of Karakuyu 3.5km SE of the site of Antioch. There's a newish tarmac road signposted to the hilltop from just outside Yalvaç. You can either take a taxi up this or walk up the old track; the hill is about 1600m high, and gives wide views over all the territory of Antioch and of the Sultan Dağları beyond. It's only a short distance from the city centre, but it's like being on top of the world; no wonder it drew pilgrims from afar.

On the juniper-clad hilltop is the *temenos*, or surrounding wall of the temple to this native moon goddess. The temple itself was, surprisingly, a classical Greek Ionic columned building on the stepped platform in the centre. Christians smashed the temple building but the *temenos* is unique, because on nearly every block of the wall, which surrounds an area about 70 by 40m, is a carving of a moon symbol and a dedication. Some stones have only one crescent moon, some several, some just initials, some longer dedications, but all must have been carved for pilgrims to the temple. Together, they make quite an impressive display. There was a *propylon* on the W and a *stoa* around the walls.

Apart from this, there's another temple and some buildings which have been interpreted as priests' houses or catering facilities, for the festivals were probably accompanied by al fresco banquets. Why not? You'd need a good meal after trudging up the hill.

There's also the remains of a church nearby but you can ignore it since it somehow spoils the hedonistic atmosphere.

SETTING UP AND USING A GPS 10.1

System Setup

All the points on the lists in the route section and on the website were taken on a Garmin Trek GPS. Before you use your own GPS, you should change the settings to match the ones we used.

System setup:

Mode: Normal

Offset: +2.00 (difference in hrs between Turkish time and GMT)

Navigation setup:

Position format: hddd.dddd (degrees in decimal format)

Map datum: WGS 84

Units: Distance - Metric, Height - meters, Pressure - millibars, Angle - degrees

North ref: Mag 004° E

Waypoints, Routes and Maps:

There are a total of about 4000 waypoints split up by day, as in the book.

Some older GPS have a maximum of 20 routes; some have a maximum number of points for each route; some take a maximum of 500 points. Check what your model will allow before you start trying to load points; we suggestthat you only load points for the sections you plan to walk. You can load waypoints manually or via a computer and communication cable or bluetooth, controlled by the manufacturer's or third party software. We don't recommend any specific maps.

Viewing routes in Google Earth

If you download the .klm file, you can view the routes via Google Earth. Open Google Earth then open the .klm file. Zoom in to see the routes and the waypoints. You could print the Google Earth screens as additional maps.

Loading GPS points via a computer

You need software supplied by the manufacturer, or third party software (for Mac users, we recommend Mac GPS Pro, www.MacGPSPro.com) and a special cable to connect the GPS to a USB port on your computer; some GPS transfer data via bluetooth.

Log onto the website www.cultureroutesinturkey.com, go to the St Paul Trail section and find the page on GPS data. Use instructions on the screen to find the password and download the file onto your computer, in .txt, .klm or .gpx format. The .gpx file can be directly uploaded to most models of Garmin GPS. You can edit the text file, using Excel, to delete the routes you don't want. Then convert the file to your required format (.gpx, .gdb, or other). There are utilities on the web (eg. GPS Babel) which convert files for various types of GPS.

Set up the preferences in the software so that your computer knows how you will connect your GPS. Connect and switch on the GPS, upload the data to your GPS and check that you can see the routes and waypoints you have uploaded. Finally, copy your software and data to a flash disk and bring it and the cable with you. Then you can re-load your GPS if required.

10.2 TURKISH FOR TREKKERS

Turkish uses a European character set (minus q, w and x) plus six specials. These are: as in French Ç,ç, as in German Ö,ö, and Ü,ü, and, unique to Turkish, Ş,ş, (sh), ğ (almost silent y) and I,ı, (hard i as in 'milk'). Each consonant is sounded separately. C,c is pronounced j as in 'jam', j is pronounced as in 'Jules'.

Vowel harmony makes Turkish musical; hard vowels (a,ı,o,u) are formed at the front of the mouth and soft vowels (e,i,ö,ü) at the back. All vowels are spoken with a short sound. Endings are normally from the same group as the last vowel in the stem.

Verb endings give person (I, you, he, she), tense (future, present, etc) and voice (active, passive). Noun endings give case (subject, object, etc) and possessives (by adding ı/sı, i/si, u/ su. ü/sü). Add ler/lar to nouns to make plural and lı/li/lu/lü where appropriate to make an adjective. There is no gender and no word for 'the'.

Take a tiny pocket dictionary with you; you can buy one in Turkey. People are impressed when a foreigner has bothered to learn any of their language - even a few words help.

(we have included a few Latin/Greek/Persian words in italics)

Basic Verbs
Hard vowels - ending (mak)
ol- be, exist; al- take; kal- stay; dur- stop; sap- turn; kalk- get up; otur- sit; yat- lie down; konuş- talk; sor- ask; kat- add/put on; çık- go out; anla- understand; anlat- tell; bak- look; koş- run.
Soft vowels - ending (mek)
gör- see; göster- show; dön- turn; yürü- walk; git- go; gel- come; ver- give; ye- eat; iç- drink; sigara iç- smoke; iste- want; tarif et- direct; geri dön- turn back; pişir- cook; temizle- clean
Adding endings
gelin, geliniz - you come; sorun, soruyoruz - you ask, we ask
Add -ma/-me to give the negative
alma - don't take; almayın - don't you take; sigara içmem - I don't smoke; anlatma - don't tell verme - don't give; gelmem - I won't come; yemeyin - don't you eat; dönme - don't turn
Future
kalacağım - I will stay; yürüceksin - you will walk; göreceğiz - we will see; soracaksınız - you (pl) will ask; durmayacağım - I won't stop; gitmeyeceğiz - we won't go
Questions
ne zaman? - when?; nerede? - where?; nasıl? - how?; neden, niçin? - why?; kaç tane? - how many?; ne kadar? - how much?; kim? - who; kimin? - whose?
ne istiyorsunuz? - what do you want?; adınız nedir? - what's your name?
nerelisiniz/memleket? - where are you from?
bu nedir? - what's this?; saat kaç? - what's the time?
Add -mı/mi to make a question:
kızınız mı?- is this your girl (daughter)?; soracağımız mı? - shall we ask?;
gösteriyim mi?- shall I show you?; iyi misin?- are you ok?; yabancı mı? - is he/she a foreigner?
There is/isn't: (var/yok)
çay var - there is tea; çayım var; I have tea; çay var mı? - is there tea? çayınız var mı? - do you (pl) have tea?
şeker yok - there is no sugar; şekerim yok - I haven't got sugar; şeker yok mu? - isn't there any sugar?, Şekerin yok mu? - don't you have sugar?
Numbers
bir, iki, üç, dört, beş, altı, yedi, sekiz, dokuz, on...1, 2, 3, 4, 5, 6, 7, 8, 9, 10
yırmı, otuz, kırk, elli, altmış, yetmiş, seksen, doksan, yüz..20, 30, 40, 50, 60, 70, 80, 90, 100

People

eş	spouse
eşim	my spouse
erkek	man
kadın	woman
çocuk	child
kız	girl
oğlan	young boy
bebek	baby
anne	mummy
baba	daddy
amca	uncle
dede	granddad
muhtar	headman
doktor	doctor
avcı	hunter
çoban	shepherd
çiftçi	farmer
imam	prayer-leader
öğretmen	teacher
polis	police
jandarma	rural police
gazi	military hero
arkadaş	friend
misafir	guest
yabancı	foreigner
İngiliz	English
İngiltere	England
Amerikalı	American

Food and drink

yemek	food
ekmek	bread
pide	flat bread
Isparta ekmek	brown bread
yufka	village flatbread
şeker	sweets /sugar
konserve	preserved food
reçel	jam
kuruyemiş	fruit/nuts
fıstık	pistachio
fındık	hazelnuts
badem	almonds
leblebi	chickpeas
meyve	fruit
portakal	orange
elma	apple
armut	pear
erik	plum
domates	tomato
üzüm	grape
çilek	strawberry
böğürtlen	blackberry
dut	mulberry
incir	fig
şeftali	peach
kayısı	apricot
kiraz/vişne	cherry
sebze	vegetable
patates	potato
havuç	carrot
soğan	onion
sarımsak	garlic
biber	pepper
kabak	courgette
patlıcan	aubergine
fasulye	bean
pilaki	white bean
ceviz	walnut
bulgur	cracked wheat
pirinç	rice
makarna	pasta
mercimek	lentil
mantı	ravioli
pekmez	grape syrup
tahin	tahini
yumurta	egg
baharat	spice
tuz	salt
biber	pepper
bal	honey
bisküvi	biscuit
peynir	cheese
beyaz peynir	white cheese
kaşar	yellow cheese
tulum	cheese
yoğurt	yoghurt
et	meat
dana	beef
kuzu	lamb
tavuk	chicken
sucuk	spicy sausage
sosis	sausage
şiş	skewer
döner kebap	sliced meat
köfte	meatball
balık	fish
alabalık	trout
sazan	lake carp
içecek	drink
su	water
süt	milk
süt tozu	milk powder
kaymak	thick cream
çay	tea
kahve	coffee
ayran	yoghurt drink
meşrubat	soft drink
kola	cola
gazoz	fizzy lemonade
alkol	alcohol
şarap	wine
bira	beer
rakı	anisette

Living things

köpek	dog
kedi	cat
at	horse
katır	mule
inek	cow
koyun	sheep
keçi	goat
domuz	wild pig
kurt	wolf
ayı	bear
tavşan	rabbit
kuş	bird
yaban keçisi	wild goat
çiçek	flower
ağaç	tree
çam ağacı	pinetree
sedir/katran	cedar
çınar	plane tree
söğüt	willow
ardıç	juniper
keçiboynuzu	carob
kelebek	butterfly
arı	bee
sinek	fly
yılan	snake

Weather/iklim

hava	weather
kar	snow
buz	ice
fırtına	storm
şimşek	lightning
yıldırım	thunder
rüzgar	wind
bulut	cloud
güneş	sun
sis	mist
yağmur	rain
serin	cool
sıcak	hot
soğuk	cold
poyraz	north wind

Pronouns

ben - I, me; biz - we; sen, siz - you (sing/plural), o - him, her, it; onlar - they
-im, -imiz - mine, ours; -in, -iniz - yours (sing/plural)
benim - mine; bizim - ours, senin, sizin - yours; onun - his, hers, its.

Position

These endings denote position: e/a - to; de/da - at/in/with; den/dan - from, e.g. sola git - go to the left; burada dur - stop here; evden gel - come from the house

Combinations

bana, bende, benden - to me, with me, from me
(su bende - the water is with me: I have water)

History and religion

satrap	Persian governor
acropolis	fortified town centre
agora	market place
atrium	courtyard
basilica	oblong building
bouleterion	council building
caldarium	hot pool
colonia	Imperial settlement
diazoma	gallery
frigidarium	cold pool
gymnasium	school for boys
hypocaust	heating ducts
narthex	entrance porch
necropolis	graveyard
nymphaeum	water fountain
palaestra	exercise yard
peristyle	columns around a temple
propylon	3-arched gate
scriptorium	writing room
stadium	race track
stoa	covered walkway
tepidarium	warm pool
triconchos	3-semicircular apse
avlu	public hall
bedestan, han	merchants' building
cami	mosque
devşirme	levy of Christian children
derviş	religious follower
dinar	coin
hamam	Turkish bath
harabe/kalıntı	ruins
höyük	settlement mound
kale	castle, fort
kaplıca	natural mineral spring
kervanseray	travellers' inn
kilise	church
manaster	monastery
mihrab	pulpit in a mosque
minber	niche pointing to Mecca
minare	minaret
medrese	religious school
raya	religious minority
tarikat	religious sect
türbe	tomb

Hello and goodbye

selamünaleyküm	peace to you
answered by	aleykümselam
merhaba	hi, hello
günaydın	good morning
iyi akşamlar	good evening
iyi günler	good day
iyi geceler	good night
hoş geldiniz	welcome
answered by	hoş bulduk
nasılsınız?	how are you?
iyiyim	I'm fine
fena değilim	I'm not bad
ne var ne yok?	...what's up?
görüşürüz	see you
Allah ısmarladık	go with God
answered by	
güle güle	go with a smile
hoşçakal	stay well
yine bekleriz	come again
iyi yolculuklar	have a good trip

Politeness

Bey, Bayan/Hanım	Mr, Mrs
teşekkürler	thank you
özür dilerim	excuse me
lütfen	please
anlamadım	I don't understand
maalesef	sorry, no
hayır, evet	no, yes
tamam/olur	ok
bir dakika	just a moment
afiyet olsun	bon appetit

Time and seasons

sabah	morning
öğle	noon
akşam	evening
gece	night
gün	day
yıl/sene	year
ay	moon/month
hafta	week
haftasonu	weekend
gündüz	daytime
geç	late
erken	early
önce/evvel	before
sonra	after/later
ilkbahar	spring
sonbahar	autumn
yaz	summer
kış	winter
tatil	holiday
ramazan	ramadan
bayram	religious holiday

Adjectives

çok	very
daha	more
en	most
az	less/a little
hiç	none
iyi	good/fine
fena/kötü	bad
büyük	big
küçük	little
güzel	nice/pretty
zor	difficult
kolay	easy
hızlı/çabuk	fast
yavaş	slow
geniş	wide
dar	narrow

Place

ön	front
arka	back
sağ	right
sol	left
üst	above
alt	below
karşı	opposite
yanı	next to
arası	between
dibi	base of
kenarı	side of
öteki	other one

Trailfinding

harita .... map
işaret .... sign
levha .... (road)
sign ....
dağ .... mountain
tepe .... hill
zirve .... peak
kaya .... rock
taş .... stone
merdiven .... stairs
basama ....steps
bel/geçit .... pass
çukur ....hollow
sırt .... ridge
uçurum .... cliff
yamaç/bayır ....slope
çıkış .... ascent
iniş .... descent
yukarı .... upper
aşağı .... lower
-başı ....head or top,
-dibi ..... lower, at the foot of
ova/düzlük ....plain
yayla ....summer pasture
vadi/dere .... valley
çay/dere ....stream
nehir .... river
kanalet .... water channel
göl/gölet ....lake
bataklık ....marsh
çamur .... mud
şelale .... waterfall
pınar ....spring
çeşme .... fountain .
yalak .... watertrough
teras ....terrace
bahçe ....garden
bağ .... vineyard
tarla .... field
arazi ....farmland
harman .... threshing floor
tel .... wire (fence)
yol .... road, way
döşeme yolu ..... paved road
patika .... path
kaldırım .... paved path
karayolu ....asphalt road
köprü ....bridge
iz .... track, trail
yol ayrımı /çatal ....fork
köşe .... corner
viraj .... bend

In village and town

belediye .... town
köy .... village
mahalle .... neighbourhood
mevkii .... centre
meydan ....village square
mezarlık .... graveyard
banka ....bank
para ....money
çarşı/pazar .... market
bakkal .... grocery store
dükkan ....shop
fırın ....bakery
manav .... greengrocer
PTT ....post office
eczane ....drugstore
sağlık ocağı .... health centre
müze ....museum
kahve ....teahouse
lokantı ....restaurant
internet .... internet
değirmen .... mill
köşk .... sitting platform
okul .... school
yurt .... school dormitory
ev/daire .... house/flat
kapı ....door/gate
çatı ....roof
cumba .... overhang
selamlık /baş oda ....
      reception/guest room
mutfak ....kitchen
kerpiç ....mud-brick
ambar .... grain store
ahır .... stable

Transport

dörtyol/makas ... crossroads
göbek .... roundabout
otogar .... bus garage
otobüs ....bus
taksi .... taxi/private car
araba .... private car
benzin .... petrol
kamyon ....lorry
traktör .... tractor
motosiklet .... motorbike
gar .... raiway station
tren .... train
havaalanı .... airport
uçak .... aircraft
dolmuş ....minibus
otostop ....hitchhiking
emanet ....left-luggage

Useful objects

kibrit .... matches
sigara ....cigarettes
çakmak .... lighter
ispirto ....meths
fener .... torch
ateş .... fire
gaz tüpü .... gas cylinder
sırt çantası .... backpack
çadır .... tent
direk ....walking pole
bıçak .... knife
kaşık .... spoon
çatal ....fork
tencere .... pan
cezve .... coffee-pot
çaydanlık .... kettle
uyku tulumu ....sleeping bag
kitap ....book
telefon .... telephone
cep ....mobile
pusula .... compass
fotoğraf makinası ..... camera
güneş gözlüğü .....sunglasses
güneş kremi .... suncream
giyim ....clothing
pantalon .... trousers
gömlek .... shirt
çeket ....jacket
yağmurluk .... rainjacket
şapka .... hat
eşarp ....scarf
iç giyim ....underwear
bot ....boots
sandalet .... sandals
terlik ....slippers
hediye ....present
çorap ....socks
T-şort .... T shirt

Emergency

imdat! .... help!
tehlike ....danger
ilk yardım ....first aid
yangın ....forest fire
yara .... wound
hasta .... sick
kan ....blood
kaza .... accident
iğne ....injection
kuduz .... rabies
kırık/bozuk .... broken
iyi şanslar! .... good luck

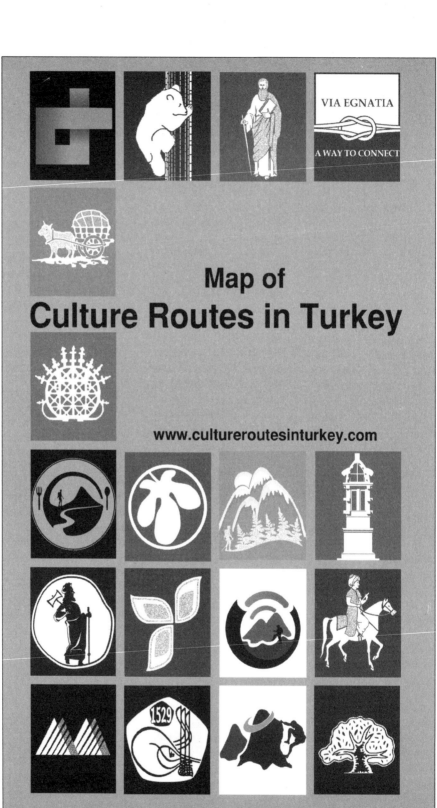

Map of
Culture Routes in Turkey

www.cultureroutesinturkey.com

The CULTURE ROUTES SOCIETY

Turkey is a huge country, with thousands of years of history, wild and beautiful scenery and friendly and hospitable people. Its maze of old roads and trails—many dating from ancient times—are now being rediscovered and combined into long-distance culture routes and clusters of day-walks.

The culture route movement is still new to Turkey, but is developing fast. The first long-distance trail, launched in 1999, was the Lycian Way, between Fethiye and Antalya in SW Turkey. Thousands enjoy this trail every year and it has inspired enthusiasts to establish other trails. There are now 17 culture routes in Turkey but the number grows every year: their locations are shown on this map, which is available on our website or at our centre in Antalya.

The Culture Routes Society was established in 2012 in order to sustain Turkey's existing culture routes, to promote the establishment of new routes, and to set best-practice standards for their development. As defined in the Society's constitution, a culture route is a sustainable route or combination of routes following a historical, cultural or natural theme. Sustainability is our watchword, and eligible routes are accordingly non-motorised.

The Society sees culture routes as a means of deepening cultural understanding—both within Turkey, where city-dwellers are increasingly distanced from their rural past, and by introducing international visitors to aspects of Turkey's culture that would normally be hidden from them. We aim to bring benefits to the areas through which the routes pass, by involving local people in their creation and by offering them opportunities to host route-users in their homes and pensions.

A major concern is conservation of the culture routes and their environment: change is often fast and unplanned in Turkey, and we will work with the relevant authorities to minimise disruption to trails where development is scheduled.

The Culture Routes in Turkey main website tells you about the Society, about parts of Turkey where you can hike and how to use the existing routes. These vary - some are mainly coastal or mountainous and some have historical, cultural or natural themes. This map and the website also tells you which routes are suitable for biking or horse-riding and shows you which routes are waymarked and signposted. All the routes have GPS points that can be downloaded from the websites. A GPS is a useful asset for independent walkers in Turkey because walker-friendly mapping is poorly-developed.

This map and the individual culture routes web sites provide detailed information about each trail and the sightseeing to be done along the way. In addition, most routes now have a guidebook and a route map. You can buy guidebooks online, at the Culture Routes Society centre in Antalya, or through stockists listed on the website.

Many Turkish and foreign tour operators run holidays on our routes. If you don't want to trek entirely independently, you could choose a self-guided walk, where the tour operator makes all bookings and transports your baggage, or you could join a group of walkers. Walking toup operators are listed on the websites; we can also put you in touch with specialist nature-tour operators. If you want advice on independent trekking, or to organise a walking, biking or horseriding holiday for a group of friends, please contact the Culture Routes Society.

All the routes give you a chance to enjoy varied accommodation—a mix of village home stays, small, family-run pensions and occasional boutique hotels. More luxurious accommodation is available in nearby towns, from where you could do selected daywalks. Older-established routes such as the Lycian Way have plenty of group walks or self-guided options, easy communications, a huge range of accommodation, and are still not over-used.

The Society has a drop-in centre in Antalya, where you can get advice before you set out, and buy maps and guidebooks to the routes. We invite you to become a member of the Culture Routes Society, and have your say in the future of Turkey's culture routes. Contact us directly through our website www.cultureroutesinturkey.com.

We look forward to seeing you on the trail.

Our centre is at:

Culture Routes Society

Haşım İşcan Mah 1296 Sok no 21

Antalya. (90) 242 2431148

www.cultureroutesinturkey.com

kateclow@lycianway.com

all the books are available at:

Tibet Outdoor

Deniz Mah

131 Sokak No 2/A

Muratpaşa, Antalya (90) 242 243 8528

www.tibetoutdoor.com

info@tibetoutdoor.com

PHOTOGRAPHS 10.4

Photographers:

AC - Aaron Cederberg, KC - Kate Clow, TR - Terry Richardson, HE - Hüseyin Eryurt, LW - Lorraine Wilson, LK - Lorenz Kober

Black/white pages:

Colour Pages (clockwise):

146

148